Discovering
Our Roots:
The Ancestry of Churches of Christ

C. Leonard Allen / Richard T. Hughes

Cover Design, Mel Ristau/Design
Cover Illustration, Jack Maxwell
Printed in the United States of America.

Library of Congress Card Number-87-72685
ACU Press, Abilene, Texas
ISBN 0-89112-006-8 (Paper)
ISBN 0-89112-008-4 (Cloth)

Learning
the landmarks and the ways
of that land, so I might
go back, if I wanted to,
my mind grew new, and lost
the backward way.
WENDELL BERRY (1977)

This life, therefore,
is not righteousness
but growth in righteousness,
not health but healing,
not being but becoming,
not rest but exercise.
We are not yet what we shall be
but we are growing toward it,
the process is not yet finished
but it is going on,
this is not the end
but it is the road.
All does not yet gleam in glory
but all is being purified.
MARTIN LUTHER

To Our Wives
Holly and Jan
With Gratitude and Love

Contents

Preface
ix

¹/Roots: Why Bother?
1

²/Our Roots in the Renaissance
11

³/Our Roots in the Reformation
21

⁴/Our Roots Among English Puritans
35

⁵/Our Roots Among New England Puritans
49

⁶/Our Roots Among Baptists
63

⁷/Our Roots in the Age of Reason
75

⁸/Our Roots in the American Experience
89

⁹/The Birth of Our Movement
101

¹⁰/Restoring the Gospel of Grace: Martin Luther
113

¹¹/Restoring an Apostolic Lifestyle: Anabaptists
125

¹²/Restoring Life in the Spirit: Holiness and
Pentecostal Advocates
137

¹³/Conclusion: What Can We Learn?
151

Index
159

Preface

Wohen youngsters grow up in a strong restoration tradition like Churches of Christ, they often raise serious questions about the church at an early age: Where was the true church in those long and desolate years between the Apostles and the restoration? When and how did the church first depart from the original, apostolic pattern? Where did all these denominations come from? Why don't people see the Bible alike, since its message seems so clear and plain?

These were the questions both of us grew up asking from an early age. To say that we asked them is perhaps an understatement. Rather, they pursued us until we finally—each of us— sought answers in the academic study of Christian history.

Hughes' first serious attempt to seek answers to these questions was an M.A. thesis he wrote at Abilene Christian University in 1966–67 under the direction of Professor Everett Ferguson. The thesis compared the ideal of restoration in the thought of Alexander and Thomas Campbell with the restoration sentiments of the sixteenth-century Anabaptists.

That thesis broadened the questions Hughes earlier had asked. First, it became clear that other Christian movements had also pursued the restoration vision, but pursued it in vastly different ways. Matters of importance to Churches of Christ were of little consequence to the Anabaptists, and vice versa. How could we account for these differences among those who claimed to uphold the apostolic faith? And second, the thesis made it clear that Churches of Christ have roots that predate the Campbells by several centuries. The question then became, what were those roots?

This question of roots took on fundamental importance and became a kind of autobiographical quest. Finally, after several years of research and armed with at least preliminary answers, Hughes delivered the annual Christian Student Center Lectures at the University of Mississippi in 1974 on the topic, "Intellectual and Cultural Backgrounds to the Restoration Movement in America." These lectures were the beginnings of this present book.

Then, in the early 1980s, Hughes turned again to the question of roots, this time attempting to assess the varieties of the restoration theme in western Christianity from the Reformation to the present. That project resulted in an essay, "Christian Primitivism as Perfectionism: From Anabaptists to Pentecostals," published in *Reaching Beyond: Chapters in the History of Perfectionism*, edited by Stanley M. Burgess (Peabody, Mass.: Hendrickson Publishers, 1986). Paragraphs from that essay are scattered, here and there, throughout this book, and we are grateful to Hendrickson Publishers for permission to reprint those sections.

In the meantime, Leonard Allen, growing up in an entirely different part of the United States and almost a decade later than Hughes, was raising similar questions. At the Harding Graduate School of Religion from 1973 to 1976, he also sought answers. At this stage of his career, no thesis helped to focus his search, but he read widely in the history of Christian thought and reflected on what it all meant.

Then, in 1977, Allen enrolled in a Ph.D. program in religion at the University of Iowa. There he wrote a dissertation which focused matters for him as the thesis had focused things for Hughes. That dissertation—"'The Restoration of Zion': Roger Williams and the Quest for the Primitive Church"—made two things clear to Allen: that Churches of Christ stand in the lineage of New England Puritans, and that even the Puritans, so committed to the vision of restoration, could not agree among themselves on the nature and shape of the primitive church.

Then, something occurred which we both count as among the most fortunate events of our lives. We two, who had travelled such similar roads, asked such similar questions, and explored such common avenues of inquiry, found ourselves working side by side at Abilene Christian University—Allen in the Department of Bible, Hughes in the Department of History. Soon we found ourselves working together on a variety of projects including a graduate level course, "Comparative Restoration Movements," which we team-taught.

The more we worked together the more it became clear that a jointly authored book on the roots of Churches of Christ was a natural undertaking. So first, we want to express in print our deep gratitude to one another and to acknowledge the great blessing of common labors in an area of study we both have grown to love so much.

Second, we acknowledge the great debt we both owe to the Churches of Christ which, in spite of inevitable human failings, have nurtured us, sustained us, and prodded us through all these years. We have learned from this heritage two great principles which have guided all our work. The first is the conviction which has been central to Churches of Christ throughout their history that the Bible is the touchstone, the final authority for all Christian faith and practice. The second principle has been equally central to Churches of Christ: the freedom of each individual believer to search out the truths of Scripture for herself or himself. These two principles have stood near the center of the restoration heritage in which we have lived our lives, and to these two principles we affirm our allegiance.

Further, understanding the centrality of these principles will aid the reader in understanding the perspective of this book. We did not write this book simply to praise the tradition in which we stand. While there are things to praise, Churches of Christ, like everyone else, are subject to shortsighted perspectives. Therefore, in keeping with the conviction of Churches of Christ throughout their history, we believe that we must return again and again to Scripture, for, as the Puritan John Robinson once put it, "the Lord hath yet more truth to break forth out of his holy word." We believe that we can pursue this goal far more effectively, first, if we know something about our antecedents in Christian history and, second, if we understand how others outside our particular movement have appropriated the restoration ideal.

Third, several people have been extremely important to the production of this book. Dr. John Robinson, Chairman of the Department of History at ACU, and Harold Shank, pulpit minister of the Highland Church of Christ, Memphis, Tennessee, read the manuscript with a critical eye and made numerous suggestions that were not only helpful but invaluable. Then, Carla Anderson, secretary in the College of Biblical studies at ACU, typed the entire manuscript and saw it through numerous revisions.

Finally, we thank our wives, Holly Allen and Jan Hughes, to whom this book is dedicated. Without reservation, they have actively supported our commitment to the task of scholarship and, more than that, they have shared with us in our search for roots in thousands of conversations. Even more vital, they have been constant companions in the pilgrimage of faith. Without their unfailing support, dialogue, and encouragement, this book would still be just a dream.

C. *Leonard Allen*
Richard T. Hughes
Abilene, Texas February 1988

¹/Roots: Why Bother?

"We need something to set against the present, to remind us that the basic assumptions have been quite different in different periods and that much which [now] seems certain . . . is merely temporary fashion."

C. S. LEWIS (1949)

W hat would our lives be like without the ability to remember the past? In an intriguing collection of medical case studies entitled *The Man Who Mistook His Wife for a Hat*, neurologist Oliver Sacks provides a vivid and disturbing answer. Sacks tells of a fifty-year-old man named Jimmy who, as a result of alcoholism, suffers from sustained memory loss. Jimmy can remember in great detail the events of his life until he was twenty, but the years after that are a total blank. And even more devastating is the fact that, when anything happens to him, he can remember it for only a few seconds.

Imagine. He meets someone and talks excitedly with her, yet in just a few seconds that person becomes a total stranger once again. Every morning he wakes up, looks in the mirror, and is surprised to see a graying, fifty-year-old man looking back at him. Every day he gets lost in the halls of the sanitarium where he lives. He cannot play most games or follow the plot of a novel or television show. Every few seconds Jimmy's world begins all over again.

Behind his friendliness and childlike eagerness there lies the infinite sadness and haunting loneliness of a man lost in time.

Jimmy has lost his past, and that loss has emptied his present of meaning and clouded his future.

Human life as we know and cherish it is not possible without memory. Without memory we lose our identity.

The Challenge

The same is true for Christian identity. Without a memory of our origins and beginnings, of the perils and triumphs along the way, and of the people who have shaped our faith, we, like Jimmy, will find ourselves wandering aimlessly, unsure of who we are or where we hope to go.

In this book, we explore the roots or ancestry of the Churches of Christ, asking "Where did we come from? How did we get this way? What has been the heart of our movement? Why do we read the Bible the way we do?" And finally, "What can we learn from those who have viewed restoration in ways different from our own?" In the addressing of such questions lies the hope of enlarging our memory and thereby gaining a clearer vision of what it means to be a follower of Christ today.

This task of confronting our past is not easy, and it may not be welcomed.

For one thing we are Americans, and this means that we partake of the anti-historical attitude that has marked the American spirit from its beginning. Those who came to America and carved cities out of its wild and pristine forests did not dwell on the past. They wanted to forget the past with all its failures and limitations. They wished to banish the decadence of the Old World, and reach out for the limitless possibilities of the New. America, they were convinced, was a new beginning prepared for them by God himself. The past was not so much to be studied as overcome.

We also face an additional obstacle stemming from our heritage among Churches of Christ. We often have assumed that our roots are simply in the New Testament and that we really have not been shaped in any significant way by the intervening history. We assume that our churches are simply New Testament churches, nothing more and nothing less. The sects and denominations of Protestantism may be products of history, but our origins come entirely from the Bible. The implications of such an assumption are clear: the recent past has scant value in clarifying who we are and from whence we have come.

This attitude toward the past has been a powerful current in our heritage. As Barton Stone, one of our most influential forefathers, put it, "the past is to be consigned to the rubbish heap upon which Christ died." To him the stream of Christian history had become so littered with "human inventions" that such pollutions in the pure waters of truth must be bypassed altogether. People must make their way back upstream to the source—the spring itself.

This call back to the source of our religion—the Scriptures—was a powerful and much-needed call. It was, and still is, the genius of this movement in which we stand.

The Necessity of Tradition

But this call brings a subtle but powerful temptation. It lures us into thinking that we can escape history and tradition entirely, blotting out the centuries that have passed and erasing all their effects. Such a process leads us to overlook our weaknesses, to think that we are something we are not, and ultimately to deny the fact that we, too, are mere mortals shaped by time and culture like everyone else.

Furthermore, when our spiritual ancestors denied any complicity in human traditions and claimed to be only a people of the Book, they partook of a profound and longstanding irony. In their zeal to reject tradition, they actually became part of a long tradition in Christian history whose substance was rejection of tradition. While imagining that they stood alone, they actually stood shoulder to shoulder with Zwinglians, Puritans, Baptists, and others who also imagined they stood alone. This book focuses on that long Christian tradition created by those who claimed to have no tradition.

Those of us who stand within this powerful tradition have tended to follow suit. While claiming to reject all human traditions, we have created and perpetuated traditions all the more entrenched for being unrecognized. Rather than escaping tradition, we who are the heirs of Barton Stone, Alexander Campbell, and David Lipscomb simply have failed to recognize the traditions at work in our midst.

The conscious rejection of tradition leads only to the development of unconscious ones. For there is a universal need for traditions even among those who profess to be without them.

We cannot escape tradition and its effects upon us. We can deny it, but we cannot escape it. We are all caught up in a web of traditions. The way we talk, the food we love, the songs we sing, the prejudices we harbor, the political views we hold, the holidays we celebrate—all of this and much more testify to the impact of tradition upon us.

So it is with our Christianity. We inherit not only the Bible itself but also a traditional way of reading it. From our parents, from the preachers we admire, from Sunday School teachers, from the books and magazines we read, we receive a certain way of reading the Bible. We are part of a tradition of interpretation.

Without a sense of history, however, we are not aware of the tradition. And it is just when we think ourselves entirely immune from tradition and culture that we are most susceptible to their influences. Unable to recognize and criticize our traditions, we unwittingly stand with our feet cemented fast within them.

"Conscious Participants or Unconscious Victims"

The challenge of examining our spiritual roots must become an important part of our growth toward spiritual maturity. Jaroslav Pelikan, a respected student of the Christian tradition, provides some useful pointers for this process. He insists that all of us are faced with a basic choice. We must choose whether to understand how our traditions have shaped us or whether to let those traditions shape us unconsciously. We are faced with being "conscious participants or unconscious victims." We can become more and more self-conscious about our past and then seek to correct its results in our lives, or we simply can deny its influence and then, by default, allow the past to keep us in its grip.

Once we begin to recognize our tradition for what it is, we must choose between recovery and rejection or, in most cases, between some mixture of partial recovery and partial rejection. That is because we begin to see the humanness of the tradition— its warts and blemishes, as well as its beauties and strengths. However much we admire those who created and perpetuated the tradition, we begin to see them as people like ourselves, as people of blurred vision, caught up in their own time and place, but cherishing certain ideals. We seek to appropriate those ideals where we can and correct them where necessary.

The process is much like gaining a mature perspective on the family in which we grew up. As we reach adulthood, we begin to see our family with clearer eyes. We see how it nourished us with love and instruction, and we learn to feel deep gratitude. But we also see ways it fell short and perhaps harmed us, and we feel regrets. We do not, for that reason, renounce our family. Rather, we seek growth or reconciliation and strive to avoid those weaknesses in our own families, knowing all the while that we share a common humanity with our parents and, like them, will make mistakes.

It works much the same way for our Christian family. As we understand its roots more clearly, we gain maturity and freedom—freedom to grow, to change, to read the Bible with clearer vision.

Pelikan also alerts us to the marks of a vital, living tradition. A living tradition always points beyond itself, never making the preservation and repetition of the past an end in itself. It does not claim to have the truth entirely encapsulated in the past. A living tradition possesses the ability "to develop while still maintaining its identity and community." It can grow, change, and correct itself. It has high regard for the accomplishments of the past, but knows at the same time that it must press on to new and different challenges. It is this healthy development that "keeps a tradition both out of the cancer ward and out of the fossil museum."

Finally, Pelikan depicts the constant tension between upholding the tradition and critically re-examining it. Without such a tension, healthy tradition quickly declines into a sterile traditionalism. He puts it memorably: "Tradition is the living faith of the dead; traditionalism is the dead faith of the living." To keep a tradition healthy means to engage in continual dialogue with the past and, through the sharpening effect of that exchange, to move beyond the limited formulations of the past.

In our heritage, however, we usually have attempted to deny or slough off the past as of little importance. The proper course is not to slough off more and more of our tradition to free ourselves from a dead past. Rather, as Pelikan puts it, we should attempt to "include the dead in the circle of discourse" thus "enriching the quality of the conversation."

Roots—Sacred and Profane

This book attempts to do just that—to help us understand our roots by including the dead in our circle of discourse.

To do that, we must recognize that our roots are multi-faceted, that in fact we have four sets of roots: (1) the biblical documents left by the primitive church—the fundamental source of our spiritual identity; (2) the restorationist side of the Protestant Reformation in which many of our presuppositions about the Bible were shaped; (3) the Enlightenment of the seventeenth and eighteenth centuries which did much to shape our rationalistic model for unity; and (4) the restoration movement of Barton Stone, Walter Scott, and the Campbells in nineteenth-century America.

If our biblical roots are our "sacred" roots, we might say that our other roots are our "profane" roots which have grown deeply in the human soil of particular times and places far removed from the age of Christian beginnings. It is these "profane" or human roots to which we turn our attention here. We do so with the strong conviction that by examining them we will be able to understand our biblical roots more clearly and live out our Christian commitment more effectively.

We begin, in chapters two through six, with an examination of our roots in the Renaissance of the fifteenth and sixteenth centuries and in the Protestant Reformation of the sixteenth and seventeenth centuries. We begin there because in this period the ideal of restoring apostolic Christianity took on the shape that was eventually to influence the restoration ideal among Churches of Christ.

As we will see in chapter two, a scholarly movement called Christian Humanism emerged as part of the Renaissance, calling for a recovery of the original text of the Bible and for holy living patterned after Christ's teachings. This movement, in turn, deeply influenced many of the Protestant Reformers, providing the foundation for the stream of restorationist thought that flowed out of the Reformation.

Christian Humanism had a particularly strong impact on Huldreich Zwingli and the Swiss Reformed tradition. So in chapter three we trace the early development of the Reformed tradition, focusing first on Zwingli, then on John Calvin, then on their successors. From Switzerland we turn in chapter four to mid-sixteenth century England where, under the Swiss Reformed influence, the restorationist impulse was sharpened and intensified by those who came to be called "puritans."

The Puritan movement, with its strong emphasis upon restoring biblical forms and patterns, is particularly important for understanding our roots. It is important because we among Churches of Christ are principally heir to the Puritans for our restoration appeal. In chapter five we show how the great Puritan migration in the 1630s transplanted the restorationist impulse to America. We will see there how leading Puritans like John Cotton and dissenters like Roger Williams expressed the vision of restoring the apostolic church.

The Baptist movement emerged out of Puritanism and, not surprisingly, continued the stress on restoration. In chapter six, we trace this theme among the Baptists in America, showing how they helped provide the seedbed of our own movement.

If the Protestant Reformation is the first of our "profane" roots, a second major one is the eighteenth-century Enlightenment or Age of Reason. We tell this story in chapter seven. There we point to the rise of rationalistic Christianity, particularly with the philosopher John Locke, and show how such views deeply influenced the theology of our forefathers, especially Alexander Campbell.

The third "profane" root of the Churches of Christ is the restoration movement of Barton W. Stone, Walter Scott, and the Campbells. In chapter eight we point to the cultural factors that allowed the call for restoration to resound widely through sects and denominations in the early decades of American nationhood. Against this background, we then sketch the birth of the Stone-Campbell movement in chapter nine, and portray the legacy it has left for us today.

The story of our "profane" roots could well end at this point. But we believe that it will be enriched, and our own perspective clarified, if we look briefly at three other stories—stories of those who stand largely outside the stream of restorationist thinking that has shaped the identity of Churches of Christ.

We look, in chapter ten, at Martin Luther who, because of his profound passion for restoring the gospel of grace, saw great danger in focusing on biblical forms and structures. Then, in chapter eleven, we examine the sixteenth-century Anabaptists, devout restorationists whose central concern was for moral purity and a church separate from the world. Finally, in chapter twelve, we turn to the Holiness tradition of the nineteenth century and to the Pentecostal movement that emerged at the turn of the twentieth. In these traditions we will see attempts to restore the life in the Spirit that marked the earliest Christians.

These three stories, we suggest, raise helpful—and sometimes disturbing—questions about our own tradition. And we need those questions. We need them to help us come to terms with our past—to criticize it when we must and appropriate it when we can.

Accepting our Humanness

Our roots, as we have seen, are both "sacred" and "profane," biblical and cultural, divine and human. For this reason, understanding our roots will be an arduous, perhaps unsettling challenge for us. Many people would like to avoid it. And in fact many do.

Thus, we raise the question once again: Why would we want to call attention to our "profane" or human roots?

We do not seek to demean the church by implying that it is only a human institution, nor do we want to ridicule the church through a cynical treatment of history. And we do not wish to disturb our sisters and brothers by calling into question cherished beliefs and presuppositions.

What then is the point of a book like this?

Simply this. If we assume that our roots are entirely sacred and not profane, entirely apostolic and not historical, entirely biblical and not cultural, then we have elevated ourselves above the level of common humanity and, in essence, made ourselves into gods.

Further, to admit our profane roots is to admit warts and blemishes, faults and mistakes. It is to acknowledge friendship with the world when we should have conformed to the mind of Christ. It is to confess with Isaiah that we are frail and undone sinners, not only as individuals, but also as a church.

And when we make this confession, we suddenly open the windows on God's grace. The gospel, after all, is God's work, not ours. And it comes to us in our weakness, not in our strength.

A church that imagines it stands beyond history, beyond conformity to culture, beyond sin, and beyond tragic misunderstandings and miscalculations—such a church has little to offer the world. But a church that owns up to its blunders and its compromises—its humanness—is a church that can both receive and reflect the love and grace of God to the world around it. In so doing, such a church contributes mightily to the restoration of the gospel of Christ.

Why bother about roots? For this reason, if none other: to be confronted with our humanness. By facing up to our past, we can better allow God to make us truly his people, not through our good works or perfect understandings, but through his grace.

Questions

1. What are two main obstacles we face in attempting to understand our spiritual roots? To what degree do these obstacles affect you? What other barriers do we face in appropriating the past?

2. What is the irony in the claim to reject all human traditions and follow only the Bible?

3. What are some of the basic choices that confront us as we become aware of the traditions that have shaped us? What risks do they involve?

4. What is the difference between tradition and traditionalism? Do you think that this is a useful distinction?

5. What are some marks of a living tradition? How would you assess your own tradition in this regard?

6. What are the four sets of roots that have shaped Churches of Christ? What is your initial reaction to this lineage?

7. How do you think an awareness of our "profane" roots should affect us?

For Further Study

Hughes, Richard T. "Why Not Take History Seriously?" *Mission Journal* 10 (December 1976):17–20.

Marsden, George M. and Roberts, Frank, eds. *A Christian View of History?* Grand Rapids, MI: Eerdmans, 1975.

Pelikan, Jaroslav. *The Vindication of Tradition.* New Haven: Yale University Press, 1984.

*Steinmetz, David C. "The Necessity of the Past." *Theology Today* 33 (July 1976):168–176.

NOTE: *An asterisk indicates those books and articles that we recommend as the starting place for further study.*

2/Our Roots in The Renaissance

"If anyone wants to learn piety rather than disputation, let him straight away go to the sources and those writers who drank immediately from the sources."

ERASMUS OF ROTTERDAM

T he earliest roots of Churches of Christ, apart from the Bible itself, lie in the Renaissance of fourteenth- and fifteenth-century Europe. This simple observation tells us much about the heart and core of the Stone-Campbell tradition.

The Medieval Background

To understand our Renaissance roots, we must recall that in the fifth century the barbarians of northern Europe shattered the Roman Empire—its political institutions, its learning, and its arts. This wholesale destruction of Roman culture plunged Europe into a thousand year period sometimes known as "the dark ages." That period was "dark" because the light of learning, for the most part, had gone out. Ignorance prevailed on almost every hand.

Spiritual life for most Europeans in that period was dominated by two themes: superstition and dependence. With learning almost eclipsed, and with reliable instruction in Scripture and theology almost non-existent, the common people indulged their imaginations in countless superstitions. The average person envisioned this world as filled with angels, devils, and other supernatural beings which controlled life and determined destiny.

The Roman Catholic Church came to dominate both European politics and culture, and virtually every person depended on the church for eternal salvation. On the one hand, the church controlled and administered the seven sacraments which, it maintained, were the only means by which the saving grace of God might be dispensed. On the other hand, the church held the immense power of excommunication, which barred heretics and sinners from the saving grace of the sacraments, and the power of the interdict by which the Pope might bar from the sacraments an entire nation or people. These powerful tools rendered an entire European populace dependent on a wrathful God who expressed the divine will solely through the Roman church.

Undergirding the sense of dependence was the feudal system. Feudal lords required service of their vassals; the vassals, in turn, depended on their lords for the very means of life itself. Since the feudal economy was based not on money or trade but on services rendered for protection and livelihood, serfs and vassals were locked into an iron system of dependence. This dominant socio-political system helped shape the common idea of God as a glorified feudal lord.

During the latter years of this period, Thomas Aquinas (1225/27–1274) helped develop a system of theology known as Scholasticism. Aquinas sought to apply the insights of Aristotelian philosophy to medieval ecclesiastical thought. His system was highly rationalistic and helped spawn, in the waning years of the Middle Ages, a bureaucracy of churchmen and theologians essentially uninformed by Scripture but given instead to disputation, traditionalism, and arguments based on cleverness and the creative use of syllogisms.

By the dawn of the Renaissance (c. 1300), then, Christianity in Europe ran in two widely divergent streams. On the one hand, a world-view informed by superstition and dependence on a feudal God controlled the lives of most common people. On the other hand, privileged churchmen and theologians indulged themselves in Scholastic disputations almost wholly unrelated to the lives of the common people. In both instances, Scripture was essentially a closed and forgotten book.

Certainly there were exceptions to these two dominant streams. Various orders of monks and nuns sought spiritual renewal, and radical sectarians raised their voices for reform and, in some instances, for restoration of primitive Christianity. In this latter category were dissenters like John Wyclif (1328–1384) in England and John Hus (1373–1415) in Bohemia. Both men called for simple piety based on Scripture and the example of the primitive church, and both sought to place Scripture in the hands of the common people.

The great engine of medieval Catholicism, however, squelched their voices, burned Hus at the stake, and forced their followers—Lollards and Hussites—into a long, underground existence.

For this reason, an effort to trace the ancestry of Churches of Christ finds few tangible roots in the Middle Ages. Many radical dissenters did indeed anticipate at least some of what Churches of Christ believe and teach. But because the Roman Church either persecuted these groups out of existence or drove them underground, one can establish no clear links that might tie modern Churches of Christ with these earlier dissenting groups.

The attempt to trace the roots of Churches of Christ must begin, instead, with the widespread Renaissance impulse to recover the wisdom of the ancient world.

The Renaissance

The Renaissance began in the fourteenth century when a new individualism among Europeans eroded the sense of dependence on feudal lords that had dominated Europe for so long. This new individualism lay at the very heart of the Renaissance and expressed itself principally as faith in the natural reasoning ability and creativity of humankind. Art, literature, music, and scholarship of all kinds flourished during this period (1300–1517).

In religion, the spirit of the Renaissance prompted a profound sense of self-reliance. Few Renaissance thinkers looked to a sovereign God to empower them to do the good. Instead, a person chose freely to do good and achieved this end through rigorous and determined effort.

The essential question of the Renaissance became, therefore, what is the good? Renaissance thinkers nearly unanimously

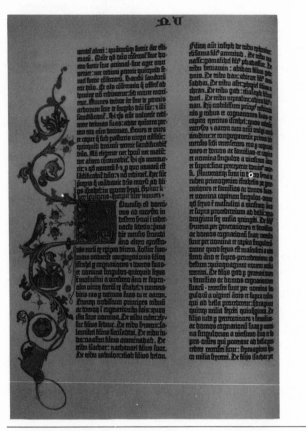

A page from the first printed book, the Gutenberg Bible of 1456. Printing exerted a powerful influence on the rise of Christian Humanism. (courtesy of Abilene Christian University Library)

rejected medieval values. They felt medieval history had polluted the stream of learning, knowledge, and culture. If one would know the good, therefore, one must avoid the teachings of recent thinkers and return instead to the fountainhead of wisdom and learning—the teachings of the ancients.

Their quest for the wisdom of the ancient world, known as Humanism, began in renaissance Italy. The universal watchword of Humanism was *ad fontes*—back to the fountain or the source. Humanism itself was a kind of restoration movement, advocating a return to the wisdom of a purer and nobler age.

The Italian Humanists concerned themselves especially with the wisdom of the ancient pagans of Greece and Rome, people like

Plato, Seneca, and Cicero. They dedicated themselves to two tasks. First, they painstakingly sifted through libraries near and far, searching for ancient manuscripts that might shed new light on the teachings of the ancients. Second, they sought to live lives, and encourage others to live lives, based on the ethical teachings of the ancient thinkers they so much admired.

Christian Humanism

In the fifteenth century Humanism crossed the Alps from Italy into northern Europe. There Humanism took on a decidedly Christian cast, producing not just Humanists but Christian Humanists. Like the Italian Humanists, these scholars sought recovery of ancient wisdom. But they concerned themselves not so much with pagan as with Christian thinkers. They sifted through Europe's libraries and monasteries for ancient texts of both biblical books and early Christian writings. The acknowledged "Prince of the Christian Humanists" was Erasmus of Rotterdam (1466–1536) whose signal achievement, a production of a reliable text of the Greek New Testament, symbolized the aspirations of the age.

Christian Humanists also sought to restore to Christendom the piety and ethical behavior taught by Jesus, the Apostles, and the early church. From their perspective, the Scholastic theologians, with their arid and sterile disputations and their neglect of Scripture, impeded piety on every hand.

Christian Humanists launched a frontal assault on late medieval Scholasticism, and Scholastic theologians responded in kind. The ensuing battle pitched Scholastics, who defended the traditions of medieval theology, against Christian Humanists, who pointed people beyond those traditions to the very source of Christian learning—Scripture itself.

A story told by Thomas More, the prominent English churchman and humanist, captures the problems the Christian Humanists encountered in the mindset of the Scholastic theologians. An Italian merchant gave a dinner party and among the guests was a particularly obnoxious Scholastic theologian. Regardless of what anyone said on any subject during the course of the evening, the theologian wanted to argue and propound syllogisms. Finally, the merchant drew the theologian into a discussion of religion.

Suspecting the theologian knew absolutely nothing about the Bible, the merchant began fabricating passages of Scripture and ascribing them to particular biblical texts, citing book, chapter, and verse. He even made it a point, More relates, "if the book had only sixteen chapters, to quote from the twentieth."

The theologian found himself in difficult straits. He had "absolutely no idea of the contents of Holy Writ," More writes. He didn't want to appear stupid and uninformed, nor did he want to admit defeat. Therefore,

> as soon as any nonexistent passage from Scripture was cited against him, he said "well quoted, sir, but I understand the text in this way," and then he would interpret it in two ways, one of which supported his opponent, the other of which provided his own means of escape. And if the merchant pressed the point more closely, and objected that the theologian's was not the true meaning, then this man swore so solemnly that anyone might have believed him, that Nicholas of Lyra interpreted it in this way.

Such was the state of affairs among Scholastic theologians by the dawn of the sixteenth century.

Erasmus spoke for most of the Christian Humanists of his age when he assailed the Scholastic theologians with biting severity.

> You may often find more true authentic wisdom in one obscure individual, generally thought simple-minded and half crazy, ... whose mind has ... been taught ... by the heavenly spirit of Christ, than in many strutting characters acting the theologian, three or four times Doctor So-and-So, blown up with their Aristotle and stuffed full of learned definitions, conclusions, and propositions.

Then Erasmus pointed beyond contemporary theologians to the true source of Christian learning and piety, the Scriptures.

> Why devote the greater part of life to Averroes rather than to the Gospels? Why spend nearly all of life on the ordinances of men and on opinions in contradiction with themselves? The latter, in fact, may now be the views of the more eminent theologians, if you please; but certainly the first steps of the great theologian in the days to come will be in these authors [of Holy Scripture] . . . . Let us all, therefore, with our whole heart covet this literature, let us embrace it, let us continually occupy ourselves with it, let us fondly kiss it, at length let us die in its embrace, let us be transformed in it, since indeed studies are transmuted into morals.

Again, Erasmus argued in the same vein that "if anyone wants to learn piety rather than disputation, let him straight away go to the sources and those writers who drank immediately from the sources."

Erasmus of Rotterdam, the "Prince of Christian Humanists," at age 54. (drawing by Albrecht Dürer, 1520)

For Christian Humanists, the theology of the Middle Ages, with its abstract bent and emphasis on logical disputation, had simply diverted Christianity from its primary goal: the attainment of a Christ-like life. By restoring the pure sources of faith, therefore, Erasmus sought to recover the forgotten "philosophy of Christ" and to stir people up to true piety and holiness. The prime source for this spiritual life was the Bible, which he called "the hidden storehouse of everlasting wisdom."

Many Scholastic theologians, wedded to the thought of their own day and reluctant to change their perspective, viciously attacked the Christian Humanists for proposing things that were "new." Erasmus, however, hurled their charges back and accused them of being badly confused. They were calling "'new' the things

that are the oldest of all, and they call 'old' what is really new."
Then Erasmus told them what was really new.

> It is something new, to exclude from the Holy of Holies of Theology
> anyone who has not sweated for years over Averroes and Aristotle. It is
> something new to stuff young men, who are reading for a degree in
> Philosophy, with Sophistical nonsense and fabricated problems, mere
> brain-teasers . . . . It is something new to exclude any arguments which are
> brought from the sources of Holy Scripture, and only accept those which
> are taken from Aristotle, from the Decretals, from the determinations of the
> Schoolmen, from the glosses of the professors of papal law, or from prece-
> dents (inane for the most part) distorted from Roman law. If we are to be
> offended by what is new, these are the really new things.

Then Erasmus pointed them to what was truly old: the
teachings of Jesus, the Apostles, and the earliest Christians.

Conclusions

One must not suppose, however, that Christian Humanists
were pietists with a strongly anti-intellectual bent who viewed all
learning as a serious threat to true spirituality. Nothing could be
further from the truth.

The Christian Humanists were serious scholars who possessed extraordinary learning. The real choice for the Christian
Humanists, therefore, was not between learning and ignorance
but between Scholasticism and Scripture. Erasmus made clear his
commitment to Christian learning when he criticized "an attempt
to interpret Divine Scripture . . . by one who was unschooled and
ignorant of Greek, Latin, and Hebrew, and of the whole of
antiquity—things without which it is not only stupid, but impi-
ous, to take on oneself to treat the mysteries of Theology." And yet
he confessed with great sadness that "this is done everywhere by
numbers of people, who have learnt some trivial syllogisms and
childish sophistries and then, heavens above, what will they not
dare? What will they not teach?"

Neither should one suppose from what has been said that
Christian Humanists typically favored the restoration of the
primitive church. Again, this is not true.

The Christian Humanists did not constitute a sect or a
church, nor did they share a uniform theological position. Some
became Protestants, to be sure, though many others remained
Roman Catholics throughout their lives. Typically, their concern

was not to recover the primitive church but simply to restore the teachings of the ancient Christians and to learn from them the meaning of authentic Christian living and true spirituality.

Thus, Erasmus, for all his criticism of the Scholastic theologians, and for all his ridicule of the abuses in the Church, remained a loyal son of the pope until the very end. He believed, in fact, that even if one could reconstruct a precise New Testament model of the church—which he doubted—it would not be suitable for imitation in the present because conditions had changed.

For all of this, however, the Christian Humanists laid an exceedingly firm and broad foundation for those who, in later years, would seek to restore the primitive church. That foundation consisted in their insistence that the ancient Christian faith was normative, and that the speculations of recent theologians were not.

During the waning years of the fifteenth century and the early years of the next, the Humanist perspective on the ancient world and the ancient Christian faith came more and more to dominate various European universities. Several persons who would become leaders in the Protestant Reformation attended those universities, imbibed the Humanist spirit, and developed a strong allegiance to ancient models and norms. Some of those reformers then channeled their reverence for ancient morals and piety into a zeal for the primitive Christian church in all its various dimensions. To these reformers we turn in the next chapter.

Questions

1. Why is it not really possible to trace the roots of Churches of Christ to medieval dissenting movements like Lollards (followers of Wyclif) and Hussites (followers of Hus)?

2. Explain the two chief characteristics of spiritual life for most common people in Europe during the Middle Ages.

3. Explain the chief characteristics of the Renaissance.

4. Distinguish between Humanism in Italy, on the one hand, and Christian Humanism in Northern Europe, on the other. What did these two movements share in common? How did they differ?

5. In what ways did the Christian Humanists differ from the Scholastic theologians of the late Middle Ages? How did these two traditions differ regarding the values they placed on antiquity and modernity?

6. Did Christian Humanists typically seek to recover the primitive church? What contribution did they make to that ideal?

For Further Study

Aston, Margaret E. "The Northern Renaissance." In *The Meaning of the Renaissance and Reformation*. Edited by Richard L. DeMolen. Boston: Houghton Mifflin, 1974. (This essay was especially helpful in the preparation of this chapter.)

Bainton, Roland H. *Erasmus of Christendom*. New York: Scribners, 1969.

*Friesen, Abraham. "The Impulse Toward Restitutionist Thought in Christian Humanism." *Journal of the American Academy of Religion* 44 (March 1976):29–45.

Harbison, E. Harris. *The Christian Scholar in the Age of the Reformation*. New York, 1958; reprint ed., Grand Rapids, MI: Eerdmans, 1984.

Kristeller, Paul O. *Renaissance Thought: The Classic, Scholastic, and Humanist Strains*. New York: Harper and Row, 1961.

3/Our Roots in The Reformation

"The clear and pure light, the Word of God, has been dimmed, confused and diluted with human principles and teachings so that all those who call themselves Christians do not know the divine will. They only have their self-invented worship, holiness, and external spiritual knowledge which is man-made."

HULDREICH ZWINGLI (1523)

While Churches of Christ have insisted over the years that they are not Protestants but only Christians, their roots nonetheless reach back into the Protestant Reformation of the sixteenth century. What was the Reformation and how did it shape the heritage in which we stand? This chapter seeks to answer these questions.

If the Renaissance was a time of intellectual and cultural renewal throughout Europe, the Protestant Reformation was a time of great renewal for European Christianity. This quest for renewal arose out of the widespread feeling that the medieval church had allowed its traditions to clutter the way to God with fees and human regulations and thus to subvert the gospel of Christ.

But in this quest the Reformation was not monolithic. It was, rather, made up of at least three currents, each with a somewhat different emphasis, one centered in Germany, another in Switzerland, and a third in England. The three movements shared some basic concerns, but each developed its own distinctive shape. For this reason, some have suggested that we should speak of "patterns of reformation" rather than simply of *the* Reformation.

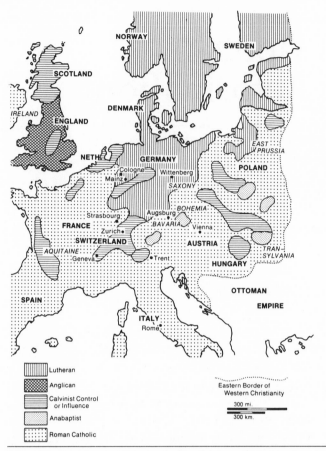

Map of Europe showing the geographic divisions of Christendom in Europe by 1550. (Yale University Press)

To trace our own roots in this period, we will focus on one of these patterns, that which emerged in Switzerland and came to be called the Reformed tradition. Before we do that, however, we first must look further at the heart of the Reformation's protest and at how the different patterns began to emerge.

"Scripture Alone"

At the heart of the Reformation was a new understanding of the authority of the Bible. Across Europe in the 1520s and 1530s there arose a fresh and vigorous appeal to the Bible, an appeal given force by the work of the Christian Humanists with their call, "Back to the sources."

It was not simply that the Reformers began using the Bible as an authority for their faith, for the medieval church had had high regard for the Bible too. What was new, rather, was the assertion of the principle of "Scripture alone." This assertion opened a gulf between the Roman Church and the Reformers by denying the authority of church tradition and the authority of the pope.

This insistence on Scripture as the sole authority had revolutionary implications. It meant a rejection of the church tradition that, in practice if not in theory, had assumed predominance over Scripture. It meant, in short, a break with Rome. For Martin Luther in Germany that break came at the Diet of Worms in 1521 when he proclaimed: "Unless I am convinced by Scripture and plain reason—I do not accept the authority of popes and councils, for they have contradicted each other—my conscience is captive to the Word of God."

The cry of "Scripture alone" soon became the rallying cry of the Protestant Reformation. This principle became central in the protests of a wide range of sixteenth-century reformers, and its importance would be difficult to exaggerate.

But as the Reformers soon discovered, it was one thing to insist on "Scripture alone" and entirely another to settle on what that meant for the life and shape of the church. From the beginning there were differences over how the principle was to be understood and applied. And as the Reformation progressed these differences exerted profound effects.

Two of the major streams of Protestant thought were the Lutheran and the Reformed. These two traditions used distinct approaches to the renewal of the church. The Lutheran approach we will call "reformation." It sought to reform and purify the historic, institutional church while at the same time preserving as much of the tradition as possible. The Reformed approach we will call "restoration." It sought to restore the essence and form of the primitive church based on biblical precedent and example; tradition received scant respect.

These two traditions—the Lutheran and the Reformed— both began with the doctrine of "Scripture alone," but each understood and applied it differently. Does the Bible provide a complete blueprint for all time laying out the details of church government, forms of worship, and rules for behavior? Or does it rather provide a central core of saving truth, leaving many of the details to human discretion and the changing circumstances of time and place? Broadly speaking, early Reformed theologians answered "yes" to the first question, while Luther and his successsors affirmed the second.

Luther was not concerned primarily with the question, "What is the biblical pattern that we should imitate?" He confronted rather the query, "How can we find forgiveness of sins?" The Reformed theologians, in contrast, returned again and again to the Bible as a blueprint or pattern for careful imitation. They were much more concerned with jettisoning traditional forms and practices and replacing them with those found in Scripture.

To find our roots in the Reformation we must turn, therefore, to the Reformed tradition with its stress on biblical precedent and form.

Zwingli and the Reformed Tradition

Christian Humanism helped shape the thought of many Protestant reformers. Significantly, those most deeply influenced by Christian Humanism were the ones who moved most readily toward a restorationist understanding of church renewal. Huldreich Zwingli (1484–1531), the founder of Reformed theology, provides the clearest example of this pattern of thought.

As a youth Zwingli received a strong classical education, studying under some of the noted humanist scholars of his day. He fell in love with the "new learning" and eventually completed a master's degree at the University of Basel. In 1506, at age twenty-two, Zwingli became a Roman Catholic priest and until 1518 served as a parish priest.

In 1516 Zwingli began to look solely to the Bible for doctrinal authority. Of his theological development during this period, he wrote:

> In my youth I devoted myself as much to human learning as did others my age. Then [in 1516], I undertook to devote myself entirely to the Scriptures, and the conflicting philosophy and theology of the schoolmen constantly presented difficulties. But eventually I came to the conclusion—led thereto by the Scriptures—and decided "You must drop all that and learn God's will directly from his own Word."

Huldreich Zwingli: father of the Swiss Reformation who put great stress on following biblical precedent. (painting by Schlesinger, 1817; courtesy of Everett Ferguson, Abilene, TX)

Zwingli's elevation of the Bible sprang from his increasing use of the tools of Christian Humanism. During this period of intense study he mastered New Testament Greek, began to learn biblical Hebrew, studied Erasmus' *Paraphrases* on the New Testament, and read the Greek classics and early Church Fathers. The result was a growing conviction that many of the practices of Roman Catholicism were without foundation and that the gospel, in contrast, was simple and clear.

It was this growing conviction that sparked the Swiss Reformation. In 1519 Zwingli became the preacher for the great cathedral church in Zurich. To everyone's surprise, he began his preaching by putting aside the prescribed homilies and preaching through the Gospel of Matthew. And during the next twelve years Zwingli continued to preach his way through the New Testament.

An understanding of Zwingli and the Swiss Reformation requires a further look at the influence of Erasmus and Christian Humanism. In the early years of Zwingli's career he was a thoroughgoing disciple of Erasmus, and this was to shape his theology in important ways.

Erasmus' concern for the past had a double focus. He had sought to restore both the ancient "philosophy of Christ" and many of the fundamentally secular ideals of classical antiquity. Both emphases deeply influenced Zwingli, but it was particularly the influence of this secular dimension of Erasmus' thought that distinguished Zwingli's pilgrimage from that of Luther in Germany.

Notice the contrast between Luther and Zwingli. Luther began with the agonizing problem of a guilty conscience, a conscience formed from within the tradition of the medieval church. Above all he sought forgiveness of sin, freedom from guilt, and peace with God. Once he discovered the good news of God's grace, he sought, so far as possible, to promote spiritual reformation within the traditional structures of the Roman Church. He instituted changes, to be sure, but he sought to preserve as much as possible of the tradition.

Zwingli made a different pilgrimage. Though a parish priest, he had traveled the path of the humanist "philosophy of Christ." Unlike Luther, he made no clear distinction between a spiritual reformation and an institutional one. As a result, Zwingli tended to see in the Bible a normative pattern for all aspects of church life.

Further, though influenced profoundly by Erasmus and Christian Humanism, Zwingli went beyond Erasmus. By 1522, Zwingli had replaced Erasmus' somewhat nebulous "philosophy of Christ" with the more structured "law of Christ." For Zwingli God became the lawgiver who "rises in the night ... to arrange and prescribe everything early, that we may not begin to labor before the allotted task has been assigned."

Zwingli came to the firm conviction that Scripture alone must be the standard in all matters relating to the church, a conviction quite alien to Erasmus. This heightened stress on biblical forms and laws and the corollary stress on "reformation by biblical precedent" was a central feature of the Reformed tradition.

Zwingli's Restoration

As Zwingli's stress on biblical precedent grew, he gradually introduced reforms in the Zurich church. Taken together, the results were striking. The ornate cathedral was stripped bare of its statues, relics, pictures, and altar equipment. The organs were destroyed, priestly vestments abolished, and the walls white-washed. The Roman Catholic mass, with its high mystery, was reduced to a simple memorial meal.

With each of these reforms, Zwingli sought to recover the primitive simplicity of congregational worship, observing that "few ceremonies have been left us by Christ." He believed that everything not based on scriptural precedent should be abolished, for "everything that is added to the true institutions of Christ is an abuse . . . . The people must be educated in the Word of God so that neither vestments nor songs have a place" in the worship.

Zwingli's rejection of congregational music provides a striking illustration. Despite his own considerable musical abilities, Zwingli excluded all audible music from the Christian assembly. He did so on the basis of the principle that whatever Scripture does not explicitly command is forbidden. He felt that audible music in public worship was biblically indefensible. After all, Paul's injunction to admonish one another in "psalms and hymns and spiritual songs" (Col. 3:16) enjoined only music "in your hearts." Zwingli found no place either in the Old Testament or the New that commanded audible music in the corporate worship of God's people.

Some of the Swiss Anabaptists reflected Zwingli's position. When the Anabaptist Conrad Grebel learned that Thomas Müntzer had translated the mass into German and had introduced new German hymns, he wrote to Müntzer arguing that "Paul very clearly forbids singing in Eph. 5:19 and Col. 3:16 since he says and teaches that they are to *speak* to one another with psalms and hymns and spiritual songs . . . ." Grebel also argued against singing from the silence of Scripture: "whatever we are not taught by clear passages or examples must be regarded as forbidden, just as if it were written: 'This do not; sing not.'"

Reduced to its most literal Pauline form, public worship, Zwingli thought, should consist of the exposition of Scripture by trained men, individual and private prayer, and the observance of the Lord's Supper. All merely human ceremonies and forms must be excluded. All practices must be judged by "the touchstone of the gospel and the fire of Paul."

Here the contrast with Luther is sharp. Though Luther attacked the ceremonial legalism of the Roman Church, he believed that many of the traditional forms could be kept as long as the substance of the gospel which they expressed was understood properly. Luther believed that Zwingli's insistence on making Scripture the exclusive norm for the entire life of the church, including its forms of worship, turned the gospel into a new legalism.

We see here an important contrast between the ideals of "reformation" and of "restoration." Proponents of "reformation" tended to stress that any interpretation of the Bible needs the very traditions it has helped bring into being. They claimed the Bible must be approached only with the mediating, conserving effect of tradition. Proponents of "restoration," on the other hand, sought a direct and unmediated understanding of Scripture, rejecting almost completely the tradition shaped by church councils, theologians, and creeds.

Zwingli and the Anabaptists

For all his stringent demands for biblical precedent, however, Zwingli abandoned his principle when it came to infant baptism. He realized that there was no explicit biblical precedent for the practice, but saw a larger issue at stake. The larger issue was the nature of the church. Was the church an enclave of professed and committed adult believers? Or did it reach out to encompass all the people of a society?

Early in his career as a reformer Zwingli considered the rejection of infant baptism, but his allegiance to the state church and its parish system prevented him from taking that step. For him, the church was not an exclusive sect but rather a broad and inclusive body. For this reason he rejected the concept of a church gathered by baptism and made up solely of adult believers.

The Swiss Anabaptists pressed him on this point. Their leader, Conrad Grebel, was a resident of Zurich and had learned from Zwingli's own preaching the importance of apostolic Christianity. But when Zwingli refused to preach and profess believer's baptism—the one ordinance that would distinguish most effectively the regenerate community of believers from the lax state church—Grebel rebuked him.

In late 1524 Zwingli began to separate himself from the position of Grebel and the Anabaptists. The reason, apparently, was his concern for upholding a Christian commonwealth—the church/state arrangement that had been dominant since the time of Emperor Constantine in the fourth century. Zwingli tried to show that, though the New Testament nowhere commands infant baptism, it can be inferred from several passages. In the process he violated his earlier adamant concern to do nothing but what the New Testament explicitly authorized.

Several scholars have noted the inconsistency. Whenever Zwingli discusses adult baptism he quotes copiously from the New Testament, but the moment he begins defending infant baptism he falls back on the argument from circumcision and covenantal continuity with Israel. The larger concern for maintaining the established order clearly controlled his interpretation. Infant baptism became, for Zwingli, the doctrinal fulcrum upon which rested the stability of the civic order and church.

In the eyes of the Swiss Anabaptists, however, Zwingli simply was not prepared to follow the ethical mandate found in the primitive model of apostolic Christianity. To take the biblical demands seriously, they felt, would have meant a break with the Zurich city council and a rejection of the power and privilege he enjoyed as a minister of the established order. It would have meant a refusal to accept the compromises and unholy alliances inherent in the existence of a state church.

But Zwingli did not make the break. He sought to maintain allegiance to the primitive church and at the same time to uphold the alliance of the church with the state. He sought to recover the rites, forms, and structures of primitive Christianity while essentially ignoring some of the ethical dimensions of the apostolic communities.

Other Reformed Theologians

The emphasis on restoration of the biblical pattern was even stronger in two other Reformed theologians: Heinrich Bullinger (1504-1575), Zwingli's successor at Zurich, and Martin Bucer

(1491–1551) at Strassbourg. Through the work of these two men, the stress on biblical precedent came to the forefront in the English Reformation and subsequently in the English Puritan movement.

In Zurich, Heinrich Bullinger continued the emphasis on biblical precedent set by Zwingli. He rejoiced, for example, in the rejection of music in worship, writing:

> The organs in the churches are not a particularly old institution, especially in these parts. Since they do not agree with the apostolic teaching, the organs in the Great Minster were broken up on the 9th of December in this year 1527. For from this time forth neither singing nor organs in the Church was wanted.

He later added: "The church should hold tightly to no other form than that transferred and established by the Lord and the Apostles and should remain unchanged." With this emphasis, he exerted a strong influence on English religion beginning in the time of Edward VI (1547–1553).

The work of Martin Bucer of Strassbourg even more profoundly influenced the English Reformation. Like the other early reformers, Bucer also stressed that the gospel of Christ constitutes the church, but he, like Bullinger, went somewhat beyond Luther and Calvin. In Bucer's view, the preaching of the gospel was not enough to maintain the church in her journey through time; one must also have discipline and purity. According to Bucer, the marks of the church are "the ministry of teaching, . . . the possession of suitable ministers, . . . the lawful dispensation of the sacraments, [and] righteousness and holiness of life." On another occcasion, he added: "Where there is no discipline and excommunication there is no church."

The discipline necessary for a pure, restored church took on a significant dimension in Bucer's thought. He believed that the restoration of the church's purity through the practice of church discipline played a key role in a nation's welfare. He developed this view most notably in his book, *The Reign of Christ*, a work presented to King Edward VI of England in 1550 after Bucer had become professor of divinity at Cambridge University. This work perhaps used the theme of restoration more frequently than any work in the English Reformed tradition. In it Bucer presented the vision of an all-encompassing Christian commonwealth in which the church, the state, and all of English life would be governed by the laws of Christ.

MIHI PATRIA   COELVM ·

MARTINVS · BVCERVS
ANNO · ÆTATIS · 53 ·
B.

Martin Bucer: Swiss Reformer who developed a comprehensive plan for restoring both church and state to the laws of Christ. (woodcut, 1544)

The ancient age Bucer sought to restore, however, was not so much the apostolic age but the age of the Constantinian church—the time, beginning in the early fourth century, when the church was protected and overseen by a Christian ruler. This ideal of a restored godly commonwealth—with stress upon ecclesiastical forms and moral discipline—was to become one of the hallmarks of Puritanism, as we will see in the next chapter.

John Calvin (1509–1564) of Geneva supplied the most influential formulation of Reformed theology. He can be viewed as standing in a mediating position between Zwingli and Luther.

Calvin, like Luther, stressed the theme of "Christ alone" when he wrote: "This then is the only means of retaining as well as restoring pure doctrine—to place Christ before the view as He is with all His blessings that His excellence may be truly perceived." But Calvin also echoed Zwingli's stress on biblical precedent. "All that we have attempted to do is to restore the native purity from which the Christian ordinances have degenerated" and to bring every practice of faith "back to its [biblical] fountainhead."

But in this effort to restore the original Christian ordinances, Calvin hoped his doctrine of Christ might restrain the impulse toward legalistic imitation. In discussing such things as ceremonies, he said that the "churches must not be too fastidious." Rather, they must keep first things first, not letting questions of form and organization occupy too large a place.

Calvin took this attitude in 1554–1555 when he was called on to advise a group of English exiles who were embroiled in debate about whether or not to use the English prayer book in their services. In this group, a party led by Richard Cox supported the prayer book and a party led by John Knox rejected it on the grounds that the book was neither primitive nor apostolic. Calvin viewed both parties as acceptable Protestants, however, stating that he prized peace in the churches above wrangling over ceremonies.

In matters of church government and organization Calvin, like Zwingli, stressed biblical precedent, but Calvin's approach was basically functional. Biblical forms were good, even preferable, but not as ends in themselves. The purpose of forms, he believed, was to proclaim the gospel and maintain the church. The balance he attempted to maintain was delicate: one was free to use any external forms that did not violate love or the gospel. Thus, he could allow some laxity regarding the particular form of church organization and practice.

Conclusion

What, then, can we say about our roots in the Protestant Reformation? First, despite our claim to be only New Testament Christians and not Protestants, we have roots that reach deeply into the Protestant traditions that emerged in the sixteenth century. The stress on "Scripture alone," the strong anti-traditionalism, the call for a return to the sources, the insistence on the right of the individual to read the Bible for himself—all of these things are a legacy to us from the Reformation.

Second, we can point especially to the Reformed tradition of Zwingli and Calvin, with its strong focus on restoring biblical forms and patterns, as one of our roots. As we will see in the following chapters, the Reformed focus on biblical form and pattern came to full flower in England and there, much later, nurtured the theological development of Thomas Campbell, Alexander Campbell, Walter Scott, and Barton Stone.

Questions

1. Why is it better to speak of *patterns* of reformation rather than simply of *the* reformation?

2. Distinguish the Lutheran "pattern" from the Reformed. How did these two traditions understand and apply the doctrine of "Scripture alone"?

3. Describe Zwingli's pilgrimage as a reformer. How did his path differ from that of Luther?

4. What steps did Zwingli take to reform the church in Zurich? Why? How would you respond to his view of music in worship? How would Luther have responded?

5. Given his stress on biblical precedent, why did Zwingli not reject infant baptism? How did Zwingli's view of the church differ from that of the Anabaptists? What do you think this says about the proper role of the church in society?

6. Who was Zwingli's successor at Zurich? What contribution did he make?

7. Explain how John Calvin stood in a mediating position between Zwingli and Luther. What dangers did Calvin see in a strict emphasis on biblical precedent? Evaluate his position.

For Further Study

Avis, Paul D. L. *The Church in the Theology of the Reformers.* Atlanta: John Knox Press, 1981.

*_____. "'The True Church' in Reformation Theology." *Scottish Journal of Theology* 30 (1977): 319-45.

Bromiley, Geoffrey, ed. *Zwingli and Bullinger.* Library of Christian Classics. London: SCM Press, 1953.

*Estep, William R. *The Renaissance and Reformation.* Grand Rapids, MI: Eerdmans, 1986.

Garside, Charles. *Zwingli and the Arts.* New Haven, CT: Yale University Press, 1966.

Jackson, Samuel M., ed. *Ulrich Zwingli (1484–1531): Selected Works.* Philadelphia: Fortress, 1972.

Rupp, Gordon. "Patterns of Salvation in the First Age of the Reformation." *Archiv für Reformationsgeschichte* 57 (1966):52–66.

Stephens, W. P. *The Theology of Huldrych Zwingli.* Oxford: Clarendon Press, 1986.

4/Our Roots Among English Puritans

"The church constitution in which we are set, is cast in the apostolical and primitive mould, and not one day nor hour younger, in the nature and form of it, than the first church of the New Testament."

JOHN ROBINSON (1620)

T he story of our Reformation era roots does not end with the Swiss Reformed tradition. To complete the picture we must turn now to England, tracing the rise of the Puritan movement in the second half of the sixteenth century. For it was among the English Puritans that the focus on restoring biblical forms and patterns reached its greatest intensity. Further, through this channel the stream of restorationist thought reached America.

Four crucial English developments help us understand the rise of Puritanism: (1) the impact of Christian Humanism; (2) the covenant theology of William Tyndale; (3) the influence of the Swiss Reformed tradition; and (4) the temporary resurgence of Roman Catholicism.

The English Reformation

Christian Humanism. In England, as on the continent, Christian Humanism played a key role in setting the stage for the Reformation. Humanist scholars attempted to set aside the dead weight of medieval tradition and to recover the source documents of the Christian faith. To do this, they studied the biblical languages, poured over biblical manuscripts to produce a more accurate text, and made new, more authoritative translations. They also attacked the religious corruption and superstition that flourished all around them, pointing to the Bible for moral and spiritual renewal.

Two men were particularly important in England: John Colet and Erasmus of Rotterdam. Colet first exerted influence in England when he delivered a series of lectures on Romans at Oxford in 1496–97. Later, as dean of a prominent cathedral in London, he preached bold sermons pleading for moral reform of the Catholic Church. The heart of his message was "the fastening upon the Pauline writings as descriptive of the pure primitive church, for a model of individual and corporate Christianity."

Erasmus also exercised great influence, as we have seen earlier. Between 1499 and 1512 he spent several years working at Cambridge University, mastering Greek and beginning work on a new edition of the Greek New Testament. In 1516 he published his Greek text, along with a fresh translation of the New Testament into classical Latin. These works became the basis for the English translations that so furthered the Protestant cause.

Humanists like Colet and Erasmus, however, stopped short of a break with Roman Catholicism. What they provided was a new mindset: the conviction that truth lay in a return to the sources and the exciting sense that a golden age of discovery and enlightenment had at last arrived. The humanists created a "preparatory change of atmosphere," an atmosphere in which Protestantism would flourish.

William Tyndale. But the Protestant faith did not flourish in England at first. Its earliest stirrings there came among a small group of Cambridge University men who began meeting in the 1520s to discuss the teachings of Martin Luther. This group included, among others, Robert Barnes, John Frith, and William Tyndale. All three later became outspoken Protestant propagandists and, as a result, by 1540 all three men had been burned at the stake or strangled for heresy.

William Tyndale is a pivotal figure in our story. A skilled linguist, Tyndale determined in the early 1520s to produce a new English translation of the New Testament. "I had perceived by experience," he explained, "how that it was impossible to estab-

William Tyndale: translator of the New Testament who believed that all Christian belief and practice should find its origin in the Bible alone. (portrait in Hertford College, Oxford)

lish the lay people in any truth except the Scripture were plainly laid before their eyes in their mother tongue, that they might see the process, order and meaning of the text." Tyndale believed that Scripture alone should determine all Christian beliefs, practices, and institutions.

In 1524 Tyndale completed his translation. It was published in Europe and by 1526 copies came streaming into England. The English authorities desperately attempted to suppress it and punish its readers, but it circulated widely nonetheless, stoking the coals of Protestantism that were to burst into flame two decades later.

The significance of this publication for our story, however, lies not just in the new translation itself. Along with the translation, Tyndale included prefaces to the New Testament writings and, in the later editions of 1534 and 1535, added extensive marginal notes. The prefaces in the first edition were based on Luther's prefaces to his German New Testament, but by 1530 Tyndale had moved away from Luther's theology. Alongside Luther's stress on grace, Tyndale laid increasing emphasis upon God's law.

In the new prefaces and notes to the 1534 edition, accordingly, Tyndale emphasized the covenant between God and his people as the central theme of Scripture. God established covenants with his people, but all the promises they contained were conditional: God's people must fulfill all the terms and keep all the laws of the covenant.

> The general covenant, wherein all others are comprehended and included, is this: if we meek ourselves to God, to keep all his laws after the example of Christ, then hath God bound himself unto us, to keep and make good all the mercies promised in Christ throughout all the scripture.

To the English readers of his New Testament, the message was clear. England was a new Israel, a nation standing in covenant relationship with God. To enjoy the blessings of the covenant, the nation as a whole must strive to uphold God's moral law.

Tyndale was burned at the stake in 1536 and did not live to see the flowering of Protestantism in England. But his English Bible, along with his covenant theology, exerted great influence. By 1538 King Henry VIII, the head of the English Church, had licensed an English Bible—based largely on Tyndale's work—for distribution to the people. And by 1547, with Edward VI on the English throne, the notion that England was a new Israel bound in covenant to God was becoming increasingly commonplace.

During Edward's brief reign (1547–1553) Protestantism made great strides in England. Official decrees abolished the mass and other Catholic rituals, ordered all images and crucifixes removed from the churches, encouraged preaching, and commanded every parish church to possess an English Bible and Erasmus' *Paraphrases* on the New Testament. In addition, Parliament approved a new, more Protestant prayer book to guide worship in the English church.

An early woodcut depicting the burning of Hugh Latimer and Nicholas Ridley, both Protestant leaders condemned by Queen Mary.

Swiss Influences. Influential reformers from the continent came to England at this time to escape persecution and enhanced the Protestant ferment during this period. Most influential among them was Martin Bucer of Strassbourg who, as we saw in the previous chapter, placed great stress upon restoring biblical forms and patterns. He assumed a chair of theology at Cambridge University and soon published *The Reign of Christ*. In it he argued that by restoring God's ordinances to both church and state England could become the kingdom of Christ.

Heinrich Bullinger, Zwingli's successor at Zurich, also exerted influence in England during Edward's reign. Wanting England to engage in reformation but not knowing how to proceed, Edward instructed his Archbishop of Canterbury, Thomas Cranmer, to seek advice from continental reformers. Bullinger responded to Cranmer's inquiry by urging England, in effect, to restore the primitive church. Beyond this, Bullinger influenced the English deeply through John Hooper, Bishop of Gloucester, who had lived with Bullinger in Zurich for some eight years and learned from him the importance of restoring first times. When Hooper returned from Zurich, he stood firm for primitive practices in the church and exerted a wide influence in his homeland.

The important point is this: during Edward's reign the covenant theology of William Tyndale was yoked to the Swiss Reformed emphasis on restoring biblical forms and patterns. Further, many English people began to view the restoration of the primitive church as the means of fulfilling the covenant, thereby preserving and enhancing the well-being of the English nation. By the time of Edward's death in 1553, many believed that the nation would flourish to the degree that the English church corresponded to the apostolic Christian communities.

Catholic Resurgence. The king's death, however, abruptly dampened the Protestant hopes. When Mary Tudor ascended to the throne in 1553, she launched a bloody campaign to stamp out Protestantism and return England to the Roman Catholic fold: During her reign (1553–1558), nearly three hundred Protestants were burned at the stake, thereby earning her the name "Bloody Mary." Her efforts, however, were counter-productive and merely fanned the flames of the burgeoning Protestant movement.

The Earliest Puritans

With the brief revival of Catholicism under Mary, many Protestant leaders fled to the continent to escape death. This group of Marian Exiles spawned England's earliest Puritans.

To understand the Puritans' outlook, we must remember their basic conviction: the welfare of the nation depended upon restoring the pure church. Mary's rise to power proclaimed a clear message. They had failed to recover the primitive church and now, as a result, God was afflicting them with divine wrath. But their duty was equally obvious. When Queen Mary died, they must return to England and transform English churches into pure apostolic communities. They could spare no efforts in this task, for never again must England suffer the punishment of God for failure to embrace the pure faith and restore the pure church.

When Queen Mary died and Elizabeth came to the throne in 1558, these early Puritans returned home to launch their intensive campaign to complete the restoration of Christ's church. They hoped that Queen Elizabeth would continue what the young King Edward had started—the drive to rid the English church of the vestiges of Roman Catholicism. But Elizabeth, instead, chose to resist the more radical Protestants, seeking a middle way between Catholicism and Protestantism.

The decisive events occurred in 1559, and came to be known as the Elizabethan Settlement. At the Queen's urging, Parliament passed the Act of Supremacy, proclaiming Elizabeth "Supreme Governor of the Church," and the Act of Uniformity, establishing a new Prayer Book as the only legal pattern for worship services. To enforce her policies, Elizabeth appointed new bishops.

Many of the now-returned Marian Exiles and other Protestants found the Elizabethan Settlement objectionable on several counts. They especially deplored the ceremonies and rituals dictated by the new Prayer Book. The church, they felt, must be purged of all such extra-biblical devices and returned to its primitive purity. Toward this end, the "puritans" or "precisians" preached in the churches, lectured in the university halls, and published pamphlets, broadsides, and books in an intense effort to publicize their cause. At stake, they felt, was nothing less than the preservation of the nation itself.

The constant appeal of these early Puritans was to the primitive, apostolic church. Such appeal was not unique to the Puritans. John Jewel, one of Elizabeth's bishops, could write, "We have searched out of the Holy Bible, which we are sure cannot deceive, one sure form of religion, and have returned again unto the primitive church of the ancient fathers and apostles." "Nothing in early Elizabethan religion," one scholar remarked, "was quite so sacred as the primitive church. Upon it hung the entire case of English religion against Rome." Most leaders of Elizabeth's English Church agreed that the primitive church set the standard for contemporary faith and practice. But the Puritans argued that the English Church did not yet conform to the primitive pattern.

One of the earliest Puritan agendas for restoration appears in what has been called "the first open manifesto of the Puritan party," a tract of 1572 entitled *An Admonition to Parliament*. This pamphlet argued for "a church rightly reformed, according to the prescript of God's word." It set out a plan for restoration based on three marks of the true church: the preaching of the gospel, proper

ꝗ A SECOND
Admonition to the
Parliament.

Jeremie. 26. 11, 12, 13, 14, 15.

Then spake the Priestes/and the Prophets/ vnto the Princes/& to all ye people / saying: thys man is worthye to dye : for he hathe prophesyed agaynst this Citie/as yee haue heard with your eares. Then spake Ieremiah vnto all the princes/and to the people/saying : The Lorde hathe sent me to prophesie against this house / and against this Citie / all the things that yee haue heard. Therfore nowe amend your wayes and workes / and heare the voyce of the Lorde your God / that the Lorde maye repent hym of the plague that he hathe pronounced agaynste you. As for me/ beholde/ I am in your handes : doe wyth me as you thinke good andryghte. But knowe yee for certaine / that if you putte mee to deathe/yee shall surely bring innocent bloud vpon your selues/ and vpon thys Citie/ and vpon the inhabitants therof for of a truthe the Lorde hath sent me vnto you/to speake all these wordes in your eares.

Title page of A Second Admonition to Parliament: *charged that leaders of the English Church had failed to accept the clear biblical pattern for church order. (British Museum)*

observance of the sacraments, and faithful administration of discipline.

In its approach to Scripture, the *Admonition* echoed the interpretive principle of Zwingli and the Swiss Reformers: nothing should be done "but that which you have the expresse warrant of God's word for." Holding up the best Reformed churches of Europe as examples, the Puritans urged Parliament "to altogether remove whole Antichrist [Roman Catholicism], both head, body, and branch, and perfectly plant that puritie of word, that simplici-tie of the sacraments and severitie of discipline, which Christ hath commanded to his church." The authors concluded that "nothing in this mortal life is more diligently to be sought for and carefully to be looked into than the restitution [restoration] of true religion and reformation of God's Church."

A short time later the Puritans issued a *Second Admonition,* declaring the English Reformation's main defect to be its failure to accept Scripture's clear platform for church order. Behind this charge loomed the theme of England's national covenant with God. England stood under the judgment of God for its failure to keep the covenant and restore the pure church.

Anglican vs. Puritan

The vigorous Puritan polemics soon aroused response from defenders of the established church. Sharp polemics marked the following years, bringing into focus major differences between Puritans and Anglicans.

Both sides held high views of the authority of Scripture and both prized the example of the primitive church. They disagreed sharply, however, about the extent to which biblical example was binding. For the Puritans, Scripture provided a complete pattern of faith and order that could and must be duplicated, while Anglicans distinguished between doctrine necessary for salvation, on the one hand, and the laws of church discipline and polity, on the other. The central core of saving truth did not change, they argued, but rules of discipline and polity should be changed to fit the needs of a new age.

The views of Thomas Cartwright, a Puritan spokesman, and Richard Hooker, a leading apologist for the Anglicans, reveal the basic issue separating Puritans and Anglicans.

Thomas Cartwright maintained that the biblical pattern of the church—set out especially in Acts of the Apostles—should be the pattern for England. When his opponents charged that his plan for restoration was "newe and strange," Cartwright retorted: "thys is no innovation but a renovation and the doctrine not newe but renued, no stranger but borne in Sion whereunto it . . . ought now of right to be restored."

The church needed restoring, Cartwright argued, because after the apostles the "government left by them [decayed and] the pureness of doctrine decreased untill the churche ytselfe (except for a few stones here and there scattered) was browght to heapes of dust." The Protestant Reformation had brought a partial recovery but had not gone far enough. Church discipline and organization must be restored, all of it patterned exactly after that of Scripture. The question for Cartwright was not "whether we have the truth of doctrine but by what way yt is best kept."

This question of how sound doctrine is "best kept" was extremely important for Cartwright, for he believed that the passage of time inevitably brought corruption. Indeed, he held that the antichrist began corrupting the church during the apostles' own lifetime and that this only grew worse in the following centuries. For this reason, he adopted a simple dictum as his theological rule-of-thumb: "That is true whatsoever is first; that is false whatsoever is later." It meant that only the biblical pattern of the primitive church could set the standard for the Elizabethan Church.

To Cartwright, that pattern was explicit and comprehensive. "The word of God containeth the direction of all things pertaining to the churche yea of whatsoever things can fall into anye parte of a mannes life." Scripture, in short, contained "a true and perfect pattern or platforme of reforming the church."

He pointed to three Old Testament "types" to illustrate the exactness of the pattern: Noah's ark, the ark of the covenant, and Solomon's temple. Every detail in the construction of these things was appointed by God. In like manner, the church had no more liberty in constructing its government than did Noah, Moses, and Solomon in building their structures. The very silence of Scripture was prohibitive. Echoing the interpretive principle of Zwingli, he concluded "that the scripture denieth that whiche yt noteth not."

Richard Hooker, the greatest defender of the Elizabethan Church in the sixteenth century, disagreed with Cartwright's approach. Hooker believed that Scripture's claims were limited. One should not attempt to regulate all church affairs and all matters of ordinary life by a rigid biblical pattern. He attacked those like Cartwright who possessed an "ernest desire to draw all things under the determination of bare and naked Scripture." "The meanness of some things is such," he remarked, "that to search the Scriptures of God for the ordering of them were to derogate from the reverend authority and dignity of the Scripture."

Hooker agreed that "the first state of things was best, that in the prime of Christian religion faith was soundest." He was uneasy, however, with the prospect of replacing human authority entirely with scriptural authority. Against Cartwright he argued that, while matters "necessary to Salvation" did not change, some areas of church affairs required adjustment as time passed. The "simplicity" of the primitive church's worship and organization, for example, suited a simple, unsophisticated age. But the English Church, officially established throughout the land and supported by the crown, required ceremonies and structures far different from those of more "primitive" ages.

Anglican and Puritan divergences emerge in Thomas Cartwright and Richard Hooker. Anglicans left considerable latitude for tradition and practical "invention"; Puritans, in contrast, sought a total return to the primitive pattern of the New Testament church.

The Puritan Struggle

From the 1560s onward the Puritans continued their agitation against all "human invention" in the worship and government of the English Church. They called upon Queen Elizabeth to exercise her God-given authority and establish the pure worship of God, remove all human ceremonies, discipline ministers, and encourage the proclamation of Scripture.

One of the most dramatic protests came from the Puritan preacher Edward Dering in 1570. Preaching before the Queen, he said:

> Look upon your ministry, and there are ... some ruffians, some hawkers and hunters, some dicers and carders, some blind guides and cannot see, some dumb dogs and will not bark. And yet a thousand more iniquities have now covered the priesthood. And yet you, in the meanwhile that all these whoredoms are committed, you at whose hands God will require it, you sit still and are careless.

Such blasts against the Queen did little to further the Puritan cause. Elizabeth stood fast against the Puritans, working through her archbishops to enforce conformity to the established church. In 1576, for example, she ordered Archbishop Edmund Grindal to suppress the informal meetings where Puritan preachers gathered to discuss the Bible. Grindal refused and offered his resignation. But his successor, John Whitgift, enforced the Queen's policy, hounding the Puritans relentlessly throughout the 1580s and 1590s.

Despite the intense frustrations, Puritanism maintained its vitality. Wealthy and high-placed officials protected many Puritan leaders, and Emmanuel College, Cambridge, founded in 1587, became a fountainhead for the spread of Puritan views.

In face of the unrelenting opposition, however, some Puritan restorationists moderated their views or at least learned to stay out of trouble, while others became more radical, opting for complete separation from the Church of England. One of these "Separatists," Robert Browne, fled from England to the Netherlands in 1582 in order to publish his *Treatise of Reformation without Tarrying for Anie*. The risks of separation were great, however. In 1593, Henry Barrow, John Greenwood, and John Penry—all Separatist Puritans—were hanged for sedition and heresy.

These Separatists understood the model of primitive Christianity somewhat differently than did the more moderate Puritans. While Puritans like Thomas Cartwright believed that the primitive church was presbyterian in structure, the Separatists believed that it was congregational. The Separatist John Robinson, pastor of the Pilgrim Fathers who migrated to Plymouth in 1620, argued that "the [congregational] church constitution in which we are set, is cast in the apostolical and primitive mould, and not one day nor hour younger, in the nature and form of it, than the first church of the New Testament."

This imperative to restore the "nature and form" of the New Testament church stood at the heart of the Puritan movement as it struggled against the Anglican establishment. Tied closely to this concern was the covenant theology that Englishmen had learned from William Tyndale and some Reformed theologians. Most Puritans, as we have seen, believed that the welfare of the nation depended upon restoring the pure church.

Thomas Cartwright joined these two concerns in typical Puritan form. The church and state, he argued, are "lyke unto Hippocrates twinnes whych were sicke togither and well togither . . . . Neyther is it to be hoped [that] the commonwealth shall flourish untill the church be reformed."

By the early 1600s, after decades of struggle, Puritan efforts to restore the church seemed to have failed in England. Divine judgment, they believed, was imminent. As we will see in the next chapter, many chose to flee England and find a place of refuge in America. There they hoped to restore the true church at last and to dwell in peace.

Conclusion

What bearing does the English Puritan movement have upon the origins of Churches of Christ? Why should we view it as one of our "profane" roots?

First, in the Puritan movement the Swiss Reformed emphasis on restoring the form and structure of the primitive church reached its greatest intensity.

Second, the Puritan heritage did much to nourish the outlook of our nineteenth-century ancestors. Our forefathers were almost all of British stock and Puritan lineage. Though they rejected major tenets of Puritan theology, they retained many of its assumptions about Scripture, the church, and the task of restoration.

Much is often made of the influence which eighteenth-century Scottish restorationists like John Glas, Robert Sandeman, and James Haldane exerted on Alexander Campbell. Yet these Scottish restorationists were essentially eighteenth-century "Puritans," neither unique nor unusual in either Scotland or Ireland for that time. They did indeed spark in Campbell a restorationist awakening, but focusing on them as the chief influences on Campbell misses the fact that they were simply conduits for a perspective rooted deeply in the Puritan past.

Questions

1. What was the significance of Christian Humanism for the English Reformation?

2. Assess William Tyndale's impact on English Protestantism and on the later Puritan movement.

3. How did Queen Mary's attempt to squelch Protestantism in England contribute to the rise of Puritanism?

4. What was the Elizabethan Settlement? How did the Puritans react to it?

5. What was "the first open manifesto of the Puritan party"? Describe its basic agenda.

6. What was the major theological issue separating Puritan from Anglican? What are some of the problems in each approach? How would you address this issue today?

7. How did the Separatist Puritans differ from other Puritans? If you had been a Puritan, how far would you have gone in dissenting against the Church of England?

8. In what ways are Churches of Christ indebted to the Puritan view of restoration? In what ways do we differ? How do you explain those differences?

For Further Study

Burrage, Champlin. *The Early English Dissenters in the Light of Recent Research, 1550–1641.* 2 Volumes. Cambridge, England: Cambridge University Press, 1912.

Clebsch, William A. *England's Earliest Protestants, 1520–1535.* New Haven: Yale University Press, 1964.

*Collinson, Patrick. *The Elizabethan Puritan Movement.* London, 1967; reprint ed., New York: Methuen, 1982.

Dickens, A. G. *The English Reformation.* New York: Schocken, 1964.

Frere, W. H. and Douglas, C. E., eds. *Puritan Manifestoes: A Study of the Origin of the Puritan Revolt.* London, 1907; reprint ed., London: S.P.C.K., 1954.

Luoma, John K. "Restitution or Reformation? Cartwright and Hooker on the Elizabethan Church." *Historical Magazine of the Protestant Episcopal Church* 46 (March 1977):85–106.

McGiffert, Michael. "William Tyndale's Conception of Covenant." *Journal of Ecclesiastical History* 32 (April 1981):167–184.

*Spalding, James C. "Restitution as a Normative Factor for Puritan Dissent." *Journal of the American Academy of Religion* 44 (March 1976):47–63.

Trinterud, Leonard J., ed. *Elizabethan Puritanism.* A Library of Protestant Thought. New York: Oxford University Press, 1971.

_____. "The Origins of Puritanism." *Church History* 20 (1951):37–57.

Vander Molen, Ronald J. "Anglican against Puritan: Ideological Origins during the Marian Exile." *Church History* 42 (1973):45–57.

White, B. R. *The English Separatist Tradition.* Oxford: Oxford University Press, 1971.

5/Our Roots Among New England Puritans

"Our endeavor is to have all [Christ's] own institutions . . . in their native simplicity without any human dressings; having a liberty to enjoy all that God commands, and yet urged to nothing more than he commands."

<u>NEW ENGLANDS FIRST FRUITS</u> (1643)

eginning in the 1620s English Puritanism, with all its ardor for restoring the pattern of the primitive church, was transplanted to America. We turn now to that development as the next episode in the story of our roots.

The Great Migration

As we saw in the previous chapter, the Puritan movement took shape as an intense crusade against the "human invention" that pervaded the English Church. Decade after decade the Puritans continued their protests but to little avail. In the 1620s they began to lose ground.

Anglican bishops, like William Laud of London, began to impose the official liturgy more strictly and to introduce new "inventions" into the church's worship. Puritan nonconformists were jailed with increasing frequency. As hopes for restoration of a pure church ebbed away and prospects of divine punishment upon England increased, many planned for colonization in America.

A small group of English Separatist Puritans landed at Plymouth Rock in 1620, but it was in 1629 that the Great Migration began in earnest. Under the auspices of the Massachusetts Bay Company, over 400 people set sail for the New World in 1630 aboard a fleet of ships led by John Winthrop. Upon arrival they threw themselves into erecting a Bible Commonwealth in which both the church and the civil order would be fashioned after biblical standards. By 1640, perhaps as many as 20,000 people, most of them with Puritan sympathies, had immigrated to the Massachusetts Bay Colony seeking to share in this grand venture.

The large body of writings left by first generation New Englanders clearly reveals the reasons for their coming to the New World. First, they sought to find a "place of refuge" from the foreboding conditions in England. Many Puritans believed that England, because of her failure to maintain her national covenant with God and restore the pure church, now faced catastrophic divine judgment. And there was the more immediate matter of increasing persecution of those who would not submit to Anglican ceremonies.

Second, the Puritans left England out of their intense desire to escape from "man's devices" in worship and find "liberty of the [Christian] ordinances." Two Puritan ministers wrote that they had chosen "to fly into the Wildernesse" because "human Worship and inventions were growne to such an intolerable height, that the consciences of Gods saints . . . inlightened in the truth could no longer bear them." This frequently repeated reason found clear expression in a later writer: "our endeavor is to have all [Christ's] own Institutions, and no more than his own, and all those in their native simplicity without any human dressings; having a liberty to enjoy all that God commands, and yet urged to nothing more than he commands."

We can say without exaggeration that the New England venture took the form of a restorationist crusade.

The Restorationist Mindset

The restorationist mindset, as we saw in chapter four, long had been nurtured in the English Puritan movement, and its importance to the shaping of American Puritanism would be difficult to exaggerate. One of the most striking expressions of this mindset comes from John Cotton (1584–1652), the most prominent minister of Massachusetts' founding generation. He wrote:

> no new traditions must be thrust upon us … [but] that which [we] have had from the beginning …. True Antiquity … is that which fetches its original from the beginning …. [If a religious form] have no higher rise than the [early church] Fathers, it is too young a device, no other writings besides the Scripture can plead true Antiquity …. All errors are aberrations from the first. [In conclusion], live ancient lives; your obedience must be swayed by an old rule, walk in the old ways ….

From Old England to New, "True Antiquity" became the final test of all things pertaining to the church. The early American Puritans attempted to demonstrate, therefore, that the churches they established in Massachusetts were nothing more than the "first" churches restored.

Because of his wide influence, John Cotton well exemplifies New England restorationism. Cotton migrated to Massachusetts in 1633 at the age of forty-eight. In England he had been one of the most highly educated and respected of all Puritan preachers. In the New World he soon became the leading theorist and defender of the emerging congregational system.

Cotton's fullest work was written about 1642 and was entitled *The Way of the Churches of Christ in New-England*. He examined the formation of a church, the admission of members, the proper officers of a church, the proper observance of Christ's ordinances, and other matters of form and practice.

Cotton believed the biblical pattern showed that a church could be no larger than a single congregation and that it must originate in an explicit church covenant. He proceeded to give a detailed description of how a church should be formed. First, the group of prospective church members examined one another regarding their doctrinal soundness and their experience of saving grace. Then they entered into a covenant, pledging to uphold the laws of God and the purity of the congregation.

Once gathered, the congregation then selected its officers: a pastor or teacher, ruling elders, and deacons. When people presented themselves for membership thereafter, they were examined by the elders, then asked to profess their faith publicly and sign the church covenant.

This way of forming churches, Cotton thought, was the biblical way, rooted in God's covenantal dealings with Israel and continued in his relations with Christians. It bothered him that the

John Cotton: leading Puritan preacher and spokesman for early New England restorationism. (Beinecke Library, Yale University)

New Testament did not give a clear example of the use of church covenants, but he had a ready answer. "In the days of the New Testament," he wrote, "the magistrates and princes of the earth being aliens and enemies to the church, the apostles thought it meet to speak of this covenant not plainly but as it were in parables and similitudes . . . ." Cotton thought that God had required such a procedure in the "purest times" and that it was needed now to keep out unconverted people who sought to find a place in the church.

Whether arguing for church covenants or against all merely human "ceremonies," Cotton sought to fashion every practice "according to the [biblical] pattern." Human beings must administer no part of the church's worship or government, he wrote, "of their own heads." Rather, they are "to dispense all according to the will of Christ revealed in his Word." All set forms of worship "devised and ordained by men" must be spurned, for "if such set formes had been an ordinance of the Lord . . . the Lord himselfe, or at least some of the Apostles, or Prophets, would not have held back that part of Gods Counsell, from the Church."

The Puritans believed that God's instructions given in the Bible were full and complete, allowing no supplementation. "The primitive apostolic church," Cotton exulted, "was . . . the most completely and abundantly fair, of all that have ever been before it, or shall be after, upon the face of the earth." Consequently, he concluded that "there is no false way, but is an aberration from the first institution."

Cotton's passion for restoring the biblical pattern appears in two issues which spanned his career as a minister, one from 1611, the year after his ordination, the other from the 1640s. In 1611, while still a Fellow of Cambridge University, Cotton wrote an essay in which he argued that the Lord's day should be observed from evening to evening, not from morning to morning as was common practice in England. He urged an evening to evening observance because, he said, it had been set forth in "the first institution of time" and thus had been "the practice and judgement of the primitive Church." Cotton's concept never gained wide acceptance in England, but it did prevail in New England's observance of the Lord's day.

The other issue surfaced late in Cotton's career and concerned music in the church. In the late 1630s Cotton and several other leading ministers were asked to make a more literal translation of selected Psalms for use in congregational singing. The work, completed and published in 1640, became known as the Bay Psalm Book. Cotton noted in his preface to the volume that in ancient times the book of Psalms had been the standard for corporate singing. This proscribed all other hymns, even those "invented by the gifts of godly men in every age of the church," as unauthorized additions to the primitive standard. With the new translation of Psalms to guide congregational singing, Cotton expressed his confidence that "as we doe injoye other [ordinances], soe . . . we might injoye this ordinance also in its native purity."

A few years later Cotton wrote further on the subject, arguing at great length against the church's right to "invent . . . spiritual

THE

VVHOLE
BOOKE OF PSALMES
Faithfully
TRANSLATED *into* ENGLISH
Metre.

Whereunto is prefixed a difcourfe declaring not only the lawfulnes, but alfo
the neceffity of the heavenly Ordinance
of finging Scripture Pfalmes in
the Churches of
God.

Coll. III.
*Let the word of God dwell plenteoufly in
you, in all wifdome, teaching and exhort-
ing one another in Pfalmes, Himnes, and
fpirituall Songs, finging to the Lord with
grace in your hearts.*

Iames V.
*If any be afflicted, let him pray, and if
any be merry let him fing pfalmes.*

Imprinted
1 6 4 0

Title page of the Bay Psalm Book, *which was the first book printed in New England.*
(Boston Public Library)

songs." Humanly devised songs, he insisted, are "not fit to be sung in the solemn Assemblies of the Church," for they lack the spirit and life of the biblical psalms. However, God had given human beings the "liberty of inventing Tunes" since he had chosen not to reveal the original Hebrew tunes.

Cotton also maintained that the use of instruments in worship, even though permitted in ancient Israel, was inappropriate. "Singing with Instruments [in Old Testament times]," he wrote, "was typicall, and so a ceremonial worship, and therefore is ceased.... [No] voyce now [is] to be heard in the Church of Christ, but such as is significant and edifying . . . which the voyce of instruments is not." In the matter of congregational singing, as in all others, Cotton concluded, Christians must recover "the purest times," for in the centuries after Christ worship had been cluttered with "inventions" that "savoured rather of superstition than of pure Primitive Devotion."

The churches of Massachusetts, Cotton believed, followed the original biblical pattern almost exactly. Some of his critics, however, disagreed. They charged that the congregational pattern "is but of yesterday, newly sprung up, unknown and unheard of in the former ages of the church." Far from being a new way, Cotton countered, it was in fact "the old way, . . . yea so old, as fetcheth [its] antiquity from the ancient of days, and from the Lord Jesus . . . ." The Puritan way, in fact, "is the same . . . wherein the primitive church walked for the first three hundred years."

Tensions and Ironies

Not only did Cotton and the other Massachusetts leaders seek to mould the churches to the biblical pattern, they also sought the same for the political institutions of the colony. The Bay Colony ministers and magistrates believed that God had laid out in the Bible the divine will for the civic order, just as for the church. Therefore civic matters, like the religious, must be shaped so far as possible according to biblical law and pattern.

Leading minister Thomas Shepard wrote that "the whole Scriptures contain the perfect rule of all moral activities." And John Cotton wrote that "the word, and scriptures of God doe conteyne a . . . platforme, not onely of theology, but also of . . . ethicks, economicks, politiks, church government, prophecy, [and] academy." Accordingly, when the Bay Colonists sought to formulate a body of laws for the new colony, they drew heavily upon the legal code of Moses in the Old Testament. By relying upon "the greatest law-giver that ever was," they hoped, as one Puritan put it, "to repaire the ruines of the dying world [by] renewing government to the primitive beauty of it."

In the free air of the New World, the Puritans sought to build their holy commonwealth on the pure biblical foundations. They threw themselves into the task with great confidence and mounting excitement, driven by the conviction that by restoring church and society to God's original pattern they would help usher in the Kingdom of God upon the earth.

But tensions marked their efforts almost from the start. At first, the Puritans saw clearly that the work of restoring and purifying must be an ongoing task. For decades its leaders had urged the further purification of the English Church. They had urged people to open themselves to a "far greater light than yet shines." And even in their own ranks, many Puritans recognized that the search for truth must be ongoing, for there was the persistent human tendency toward "inventions," conceit, and spiritual dullness.

From this perspective, John Cotton warned that though New England's churches demonstrate "a greater face of reformation than in any [other] churches," they could not "rest in Reformation and formes of it." Others insisted likewise that New England must resist the "conceit of having already attained a perfect reformation."

But the New England Puritans succumbed to just such a conceit. They soon became convinced that they had indeed restored all of God's original institutions to their purest form. John Cotton wrote smugly that the New England churches were as close as could be to what "the Lord Jesus [would erect] were he here himselfe in person." The Puritans' confidence that they had fully recovered the ancient and pure way was so great that they often sought to coerce Baptists, Quakers, and other dissenters to conform to Puritan doctrinal standards.

In 1651, for example, Puritan magistrates imprisoned several Baptists and publicly whipped one of them. News of the brutal treatment reached England and several people wrote Massachusetts in protest. One letter sent to Cotton raised a pointed question: how could the New Englanders coerce others when they themselves once had fled coercion?

Cotton's answer is revealing. "There is a vast difference," he wrote, "between mens inventions and Gods institutions. We fled from mens inventions, to which we else should have been compelled. We compell none to mens inventions." The Puritans, convinced that they had discerned the will of God on all important matters, felt divinely justified in coercing those who disseminated doctrinal error.

Puritan Dissent

A few people in New England, however, disputed these smug assertions. One was Roger Williams (1603?-1683), the founder of Rhode Island. Williams was exiled from the Massachusetts Bay Colony in 1636 because of his insistence that Christ's church not be upheld by the civil power and that the very idea of an officially established church was blasphemous.

Shortly after his banishment, Williams wrote a letter to John Cotton arguing, despite all the confident claims, that restoration was unfinished among the Massachusetts churches. Williams charged that in spite of significant progress toward primitive Christianity, "yet you never came out of the Wilderness to this Day." He charged that they had failed to break completely with the Church of England and thus to separate the church from the world. Williams advised them to "abstract your selfe with a holy violence from the Dung heape of this Earth" and "to finish holiness in the feare of God."

In the months following this letter to Cotton, Williams' intense concern for the purity and full restoration of the church led him to ever more radical positions. By 1638 he had become convinced that scriptural baptism involved the immersion of adult believers, not the sprinkling of infants. As a result, he and about ten other people rebaptized each other and together formed the first Baptist Church in Providence, Rhode Island. But his association with that church was brief; within a few months he left the Baptist congregation and evidently never associated himself with a church again.

Williams made this difficult decision because he came to believe that Christ's true church had ceased to exist. The "falling away from the first primitive Christian state or worship" had been so absolute, he concluded, that there had been a "desolation of Zion," a "total routing of the Church and Ministry of Christ Jesus." The New Testament pattern, he believed, demonstrated that churches were formed only by apostles or those directly commissioned by them.

But the chain of apostolic authority had been broken by a great influx of worldliness shortly after the time of Emperor Constantine (mid-fourth century A.D.). Since that time, therefore, no authority had remained for establishing churches "after the first pattern." Any attempt to do so, Williams warned, would

The
Hireling Miniſtry
None of
CHRISTS,
OR
A Diſcourſe touching the Propa-
gating the Goſpel of CHRIST
JESUS.

Humbly Preſented to ſuch Pious
and Honourable Hands, whom
the preſent Debate thereof con-
cerns.

By ROGER WILLIAMS, *of* Providence
in New England.

London, Printed in the ſecond
Moneth, 1652.

Title page of a tract reflecting Roger Williams' belief that the true church had ceased to exist. (Complete Works of Roger Williams)

result only in "great mistakes, and wandrings from the Patternes and Institutions of Christ Jesus." The task now, he maintained, was not to establish churches but to expose and denounce the corruptions of Christianity and to wait for God's impending restoration of "lost Zion."

For Williams, therefore, restoration of the true church was a human impossibility. Only God in the divinely appointed time could do it. When that time came, God would commission new apostles to proclaim the ancient gospel with power and gather apostolic congregations. With the arrival of these new apostles there would be a new Pentecost bringing great displays of spiritual power and mass conversions. All of Christ's original ordinances—baptism by immersion in rivers, the Lord's Supper, and laying on of hands, for example—would be reinstituted and faithfully observed.

When that time of restoration came, people would have no trouble discerning the true church. They would need no debates about its true nature and proper form. Indeed, Williams believed that the endless controversies in his own day provided eloquent testimony to the absence of Christ's true church.

Despite the collapse of the true church in the fourth century, Williams believed that across the succeeding centuries God had raised up many Christian "witnesses" to lead God's "exiled" people. These "witnesses" were heroic figures like John Wyclif, John Hus, Martin Luther, and John Calvin who held up Christian truth at great personal cost. At the same time, these great leaders had failed to see all of their false practices and to make full repentence for them. Williams noted that Luther, for example, continued to hold on to several "grosse abominations concerning God's worship," but that he still possessed the "life of Christ Jesus in him" and helped impart that life to thousands of others.

Roger Williams possessed a keen sense of the finitude of all present human judgment. Simple historical observation, he believed, provided overwhelming evidence that all "human Reformations are fallible." Seeing his brethren attempting to force "orthodoxy" upon others, he asked them:

> Have there not been as excellent and heavenly Reformers as your selves . . . whose professed Reformation you now dislike? Who shall outshine many of the Waldensian Reformers for Holynesse, Zeale, patience? Where hath that precious man been found, who hath (for personal excellencies) outshined Luther? and who shall top those Bishops burnt for Christ Jesus in Queen Maries days?

Williams answered that they all were godly people and "excellent reformers, full of zeal for the true service of God," but that their work "now seems to be beside the first pattern."

He then asked the central question. What makes present-day reformers so certain that they are exempt from such errors and limitations in judgment? The fact is, he responded, that even God's most beloved people often are "sad, drowsie and unkind" in their "answer to the knocks and calls of Christ." He concluded that his own Puritan brethren should be much more cautious in dividing the orthodox from the heretic, the sound from the unsound, for all believers have a certain spiritual sluggishness about them. All believers have blind spots that may be the object of "further light."

Roger Williams remained a thorn in the side of the Massachusetts Puritans. He engaged in intense and lengthy debate with John Cotton, his chief protagonist. Though a gentle man with "many precious parts," as John Winthrop had noted, Williams was unrelenting in his attack on the smug pretensions and misguided zeal of his fellow Puritans. He saw with keen vision just how easy it was to delude oneself into thinking that one had fully restored the true church. He understood how easy it was to let such smug certitude cloak self-serving ends and justify mistreatment of opponents.

Williams' protests had little effect in his own lifetime. He stood as a solitary "witness," dismissed as a blasphemer, a nuisance, and a crank. Only later, long after his death, would he be hailed as one of the fathers of religious liberty in America.

Conclusion

We have seen that, beginning in the seventeenth century, Puritanism flowed in two separate streams, one in England and one in America. Each stream in its own way influenced our movement. The English Puritan influence came through men like Thomas and Alexander Campbell who drew from this stream long before they ever reached America.

The American Puritan influence came more at the grass roots level. First, it established a restorationist mindset at the very beginning of the American experience, and that mindset shaped the currents of American religion and politics in the succeeding three and a half centuries. Second, Puritanism stood behind the rise of the Separate Baptist movement in the 1750s. As we will see in the next chapter, the Separate Baptist movement, with its strong concern for restoring the New Testament church, did much to prepare the ground for the rapid growth of our movement in the early nineteenth century.

Questions

1. What reasons did the early New England Puritans give for migrating to the New World?

2. According to John Cotton, what was the biblical pattern for forming a church?

3. What was Cotton's view of congregational singing and of instrumental music in Christian worship?

4. What basic tension emerged in the Puritans' attempt to restore church and state to the biblical standards? How have Churches of Christ dealt with this same tension?

5. On what ground did Roger Williams oppose his fellow Puritans in Massachusetts?

6. Describe Williams' own view of the fall and restoration of the church. What role did human beings play in the work of restoration?

7. How did Williams view the work of Christian reformers throughout the ages? How should we view them today?

8. What might we learn from seeing our roots in the Puritan movement?

For Further Study

*Bozeman, T. Dwight. *Live Ancient Lives: The Primitivist Dimension of Puritanism*. Chapel Hill, NC: University of North Carolina Press, 1988.

Bremer, Francis J. *The Puritan Experiment: New England Society from Bradford to Edwards*. New York: St. Martin's Press, 1976.

Emerson, Everett H. *John Cotton*. New York: Twayne, 1965.

Gilpin, W. Clark. *The Millenarian Piety of Roger Williams*. Chicago: University of Chicago Press, 1979.

*Hughes, Richard T., and Allen, C. Leonard. "The Constraints of 'True Antiquity': John Cotton and the New England Way." In *Illusions of Innocence: Protestant Primitivism in America, 1630-1875*. Chicago: University of Chicago Press, 1988.

*_____. "The Quest for 'Soul Liberty': Roger Williams and Puritan Dissent." In *Illusions of Innocence*.

John Cotton on the Churches of New England. Edited by Larzer Ziff. Cambridge, MA: Harvard University Press, 1968.

Williams, Roger. *The Complete Writings of Roger Williams*. 7 Volumes. New York: Russell and Russell, 1963.

Winslow, Ola. *Master Roger Williams: A Biography*. New York: Macmillan, 1957.

6/Our Roots Among Baptists

"The Church which Christ himself organized in Jerusalem is an authoritative model to be patterned after until the end of time . . . . The Catholic and the various Protestant sects were originated and set up many ages after the ascension of Christ . . . . They are therefore not divine—but human institutions."

JAMES R. GRAVES (1855)

The Puritan movement spun off several groups. One of these was the Baptists, and we now turn to this movement in tracing our modern roots.

Emerging from English Puritanism at the turn of the seventeenth century, the Baptists shared the Puritans' profound concern for restoring the primitive church. One of the early leaders was John Smyth (1570–1612), a Separatist Puritan turned Baptist. He laid out his life's course by pledging that he would never rest until he had reduced "the worship and ministry of the Church, to the primitive Apostolic institution from which as yet it is so far distant." Thomas Helwys (1550–1616), leader of another Baptist group, wrote that among all the English churches only the Baptist way of baptism duplicated the apostolic practice of adult immersion upon a profession of faith.

The early English Baptists were divided between General Baptists who believed in a "general" atonement for all humankind and Particular Baptists who held to a "particular" atonement only for the elect. They all shared the basic Puritan assumption that the primitive church should be restored in their day as nearly as possible. The Baptists, however, thought that by immersing only adults they had gotten one step closer than most of their Puritan brethren.

Early Baptists in America

Baptist churches took root in early America. In 1639 Roger Williams, as we saw in chapter five, helped establish the first Baptist Church in America in Providence, Rhode Island. Although outlawed in the Massachusetts Bay Colony, by the 1660s a Baptist Church had been established in Boston.

The Baptists flourished, however, in the Middle Colonies. In 1707 five Particular Baptist congregations joined to form the Philadelphia Baptist Association, and this organization became a dominant force among American Baptists for a century.

Concern to restore the pattern of the early church persisted among the Particular Baptists. The work of Morgan Edwards (1722–1795), a prominent preacher in Philadelphia and early Baptist historian, illustrates this pervading interest. In 1768 he published *The Customs of Primitive Churches*, outlining in copious detail his view of the scriptural name, structure, officers, ordinances, worship, and discipline of the church.

For Edwards, every detail of church life must find its origin in "the Bible, and the Bible only." One must search the Scriptures and practice only what one finds patterned there. In his search, Edwards found thirteen scriptural ordinances or rites that the church should practice: baptism, the Lord's supper, laying on of hands, the right hand of fellowship, foot washing, the holy kiss, the love feast, anointing the sick, collecting money for the saints, feasts, fasting, funerals, and marriage.

Edwards believed these ordinances should be observed according to specific biblical instructions and examples. The Lord's supper, therefore, should be observed "every Lord's day evening." Not only did the "Primitive Christians" observe it at that time, but the very term "supper" requires it since "any other time would make it the Lord's breakfast or the Lord's dinner."

In the matter of church officers, Edwards believed that the biblical pattern provided for "teachers; elders; deacons; deaconesses; and clerks," and that each congregation should "have more than one of each sort." In all matters relating to the form, structure, and activity of the church, Edwards concluded, Christians are bound by biblical "orders" and "tied to [biblical] rules." They must not go beyond the instructions of Scripture and "invent" any new practice.

Edwards hoped that his book would be endorsed by the Philadelphia Association as a manual for all of the associated churches. But not all the Baptist leaders shared his strict restorationism, and the book was not adopted. Still it apparently exercised considerable influence among Particular Baptist Churches.

The Separate Baptist Movement

Despite the prominence of the Philadelphia Baptist tradition in colonial America, our primary concern in this chapter is the Separate Baptist movement that emerged in the mid-eighteenth century. For it was this stream that watered the seedbed in which our own movement took root in the early nineteenth century.

To understand the rise of the Separate Baptists, we must look to the Great Awakening and its impact on the Congregational Churches of New England. By the early eighteenth century, the churches established by the Puritans had grown staid and formal. The standards for church membership had been lowered, religion had grown more rationalistic, and people were less given to "fervent exercises of the heart."

In this atmosphere, the Great Awakening broke forth in the 1730s and 1740s under the vigorous preaching of men like Jonathan Edwards (1703–1758) and George Whitefield (1714–1770). Thousands were converted in what was interpreted as the dramatic outpouring of God's Spirit.

With the revival came great upheaval in the established churches as bitter disputes flared and churches often divided. Those who opposed the revivals were called Old Lights; those who supported them were called New Lights. The more moderate New Lights sought to remain in their churches, but more radical New Lights advocated complete separation from all lax and spiritless churches.

These more radical New Lights became known as Separates. They sought a return to the golden age of Puritanism, to the time when church membership hinged upon the recounting of an experience of saving grace.

In the following years many Separates embraced believer's baptism and became Separate Baptists. As the movement took shape, two themes emerged: freedom in the Spirit and the rejection of creeds or confessions of faith. These two motifs were

Isaac Backus: Separate Baptist leader who wrote a history of the Baptists designed to further the cause of restoration. (Southern Baptist Historical Commission, Nashville, TN)

closely related, since a focus on the free work of God through the Spirit left little room for the strictures of human traditions or ministerial rule. The result was a blatant disregard for denominational lines and a passion to follow nothing but the practice of Jesus and the apostles.

The Separate Baptist John Leland (1754–1841), for example, said that he followed nothing but the "wind of heaven." He added that human creeds do nothing but "check any further pursuit after truth, confine the mind into a particular way of reasoning, and give rise to frequent separations."

For Separate Baptists, the Bible was the "perfect rule" for the church. Like the Puritans before them, they sought in Scripture the church's original form and structure. Unlike the Puritans, however, they left room for disagreements about the precise details of the biblical pattern, for they did not want to revert to the strict conformity they had fought so hard to escape.

Perhaps the most influential Separate Baptist leader in New England was Isaac Backus (1724–1806). Backus wrote a two-volume history of the early Baptists in America to promote "a return to the primitive purity and liberty of the Christian church." He described the long night of departure from the biblical pattern—the introduction of infant baptism, the use of "heathen philosophy" to interpret the Bible, the use of the secular power to advance Christian faith.

Through it all and down to his day, he continued, religion was marked by "endless confusion," "inventions of men," and "contests for preeminence." But a great restoration was occurring. "A great and effectual door is now opened," he wrote, "for terminating these disputes, and for a return to the primitive purity and liberty of the Christian church. To trace out the evil effects of the apostasy, and to promote . . . such a return, is the great design" of this work.

This concern for restoration remained a central feature of the Separate Baptist movement.

Separate Baptists in the South

Though the Separate Baptist movement began in New England, its most spectacular growth occurred in the South. Two men were largely responsible: Shubal Stearns (1706–1771) and his brother-in-law Daniel Marshall (1706–1784). In 1755 they led a group of Separate Baptists from New England to Sandy Creek, North Carolina, and there formed a church. Within twenty years that one church had spawned forty-two congregations and converted thousands.

Among these southern Separate Baptists, the emphasis on duplicating the form of the New Testament church intensified. According to Morgan Edwards, who traveled through North Carolina, most of the Separate Baptist Churches practiced the "nine Christian rites": baptism, the Lord's supper, the love feast, footwashing, the kiss of charity, anointing the sick, laying on of hands, dedication of children, and the right hand of fellowship.

They also appointed elders, deacons, and deaconesses, believing these offices to have precedents in the New Testament. Their writings were filled with appeals to scriptural "precedent" and to the "primitive Christians." One writer claimed that, upon examination, people would find the Baptist Church "exactly corresponding with the rule and line of the Gospel in every part of it."

In the 1770s and 1780s the Separate Baptist movement spread to the western frontier. Westward migration brought many Separate Baptists from Virginia and the Carolinas into south central Kentucky and the Cumberland region of Tennessee. There the Baptists continued to flourish. By the early nineteenth century, for example, there were two large Separate Baptist associations in Kentucky. The churches in these associations continued to reject all creeds and even the simplest procedural guidelines for their associations. As their minutes report, they sought to adhere instead to the Bible alone "without note or comment."

It is hardly surprising that the efforts of Barton Stone and then Alexander Campbell took root in those southern areas where the Separate Baptists had, for a generation or more, rejected creeds and held up the Bible alone as their guide. Stone and Campbell called for a simplified Christianity achieved by a "restoration of the ancient order," and that call struck rich chords among a people long nurtured on simplicity and a passion for primitive Christianity.

Barton Stone's movement seems to have drawn most heavily from the ranks of the Separate Baptists. One contemporary observer reported that by 1811 over 13,000 people associated themselves with Stone's "Christian" movement. Many of these were from Separate Baptist background.

Campbell's movement also drew heavily from the Separate Baptists, especially in Kentucky. Church records show, for example, that between 1824 and 1832 eleven churches and about 500 members of the South Kentucky Association of Separate Baptists joined the ranks of Campbell's followers.

It is clear that the soil in which our movement grew had been readied in part by the vigorous restorationism of the Separate Baptists who had settled along the southern frontier a generation earlier.

The Landmark Baptists

The restorationism of the Separate Baptists also stood behind another similar movement: the Landmark Baptists. This body emerged in the mid-nineteenth century in middle Tennessee—the same region where Churches of Christ had their greatest strength at that time.

The Landmark Baptists began in Nashville, Tennessee, in the late 1840s under the leadership of James R. Graves (1820–1893). In the decades that followed they had an enormous influence among Baptist churches all across the South.

If the Separate Baptists had emphasized freedom from constraining human traditions and the right of the individual to read the Bible for himself, Graves and the Landmark Baptists turned in a quite different direction. They sought to construct a precise blueprint of the primitive church, a blueprint from which one could not deviate and still be considered a member of the true church.

In his many polemical writings, James Graves had one overarching goal: "to establish the facts in the minds of all, who will give me an impartial hearing, that Baptist churches are the churches of Christ, and that they *alone* hold, and have alone ever held, and preserved the doctrine of the gospel in all ages since the ascension of Christ."

Graves attempted to support his argument at every point with restorationist appeals. Christ founded the church, he argued, and left in the New Testament a precise blueprint for its organization, worship, and practices. Human beings had no right to add or delete anything. Any church, he concluded, that was "not organized according to the pattern of the Jerusalem church" was no church at all.

On this basis, Graves attacked the many denominations of his day as heretical innovators, especially those that practiced infant baptism. He attacked all who practiced what he called "alien immersions" and included "Campbellites" among them. He gained fame, in fact, for his written debate with the aging Alexander Campbell, published under the title *Alexander Campbell and Campbellism Exposed*.

Exposing all false or man-made churches, Graves felt, was easy. One simply asked about the group's date of origin. If it did not begin with Christ in the first century and reveal an "identical

James R. Graves: Landmark Baptist leader who believed that the first Jerusalem church provided an exact pattern for all time. (Southern Baptist Historical Commission, Nashville, TN)

structural organism" to that of the Jerusalem church, it was a false church. On this basis, for example, Graves rejected the Methodist Church. "Methodism cannot justly be called a Church of Christ," he wrote, because it is "too young by 1747 years—it being only 68 years old." The Campbellite church fell into the same category, he felt, since it was of recent origin and did not measure up to the New Testament pattern.

Another Landmark leader who used this tactic with great success was Amos C. Dayton (1813–1865). His tract, *An Ancient Landmark Reset*, gave the movement its name. He also wrote a popular polemical novel entitled *Theodosia Ernest*. The second volume of the novel was subtitled, *Ten Days Travel in Search of the*

Church, and illustrates the restorationist arguments of the Land-markers.

In Dayton's story a Dr. Thinkwell has recently been con-verted to Christianity and is searching eagerly for the true church. While traveling on a ship, he encounters the Reverend Percy and Professor Courtney who are both Baptists. They are joined in their discussions by an Episcopal bishop and a Methodist minister. Together they search the New Testament and find nine marks of the true church. Then the two Baptists lead the group in measur-ing the Protestant denominations using these marks as a stan-dard. One by one each denomination falls short. Finally they measure the Baptist Church against the nine marks and it, of course, measures up perfectly.

Dayton's novel captures the heart of the Landmark Baptist outlook. The New Testament contains an exact blueprint for the church, they believed, and the many human churches of recent origin should conform themselves to that original pattern and become Baptist. Toward that end, Graves and his associates sought to confront all "human traditions, and mutilated and profaned ordinances, and those who impiously presume to enact laws in place of Christ, and to change the order of his church."

In this task, the Landmark Baptists experienced great suc-cess. With his inflammatory writing and debating skills, Graves excelled in a time when, as one middle Tennessee Baptist re-marked in 1851, "Theological champions meet with burnished swords and cut and hew each other to the wondrous gratification of their respective partisans, who gather in hundreds for succes-sive weeks to these scenes of religious combat."

By 1860 Landmarkism was a major force in the Southern Baptist Convention. Its influence continued to spread in the following decades so that by the 1880s one Baptist historian could observe that Landmark doctrines "prevail, in whole or in part, in nearly all the southern churches."

Conclusion

It is striking that Landmark Baptists and Churches of Christ flourished in the same region at about the same time and that they both took similar approaches to the task of restoration. They differed, to be sure, on the details of the blueprint, but still they spoke about the church and its restoration in remarkably similar ways.

Perhaps the similarities should not surprise us. For the Landmark Baptist movement ultimately drew its strength from the earlier Separate Baptists—the same restorationist strand of the Baptist heritage that nourished the Stone and Campbell movements in the early years of the nineteenth century.

Before we look more closely at the birth of our own movement, we must now turn to another important part of our modern roots: the Age of Reason.

Questions

1. Describe the restorationist thinking among the Particular Baptists in eighteenth-century America.

2. What was the Great Awakening? Describe the origins of the Separate Baptists in this period.

3. What were the central themes among Separate Baptists? How do these themes relate to their view of restoration?

4. Trace the Separate Baptist movement from New England to the western frontier in the latter half of the eighteenth century.

5. How did the Landmark Baptists view the task of restoring the New Testament church? How did their emphasis differ from the Separate Baptists?

6. What strategy did the Landmarkers use to attack denominational churches? What strategy have Churches of Christ typically used to attack them?

7. Why do you think the Landmark Baptist movement experienced such great success in the southern United States? Could these same factors help explain the growth of Churches of Christ in the same period?

8. How would you account for the similarities between Landmark Baptists and Churches of Christ?

For Further Study

Backus, Isaac. *A History of New England with Particular Reference to the Denomination of Christians Called Baptists.* 2nd edition. Newton, MA: Backus Historical Society, 1871.

Gates, Errett. *The Early Relation and Separation of Baptists and Disciples.* Chicago: Christian Century, 1904.

Goen, C. C. *Revivalism and Separatism in New England, 1740–1800.* New Haven: Yale University Press, 1962.

*Hudson, Winthrop S., ed. *Baptist Concepts of the Church.* Philadelphia: Judson Press, 1959.

*Hughes, Richard T. and Allen, C. Leonard. "The Ancient Landmarks: Baptist Primitivism from the Separates to James R. Graves." In *Illusions of Innocence: Protestant Primitivism in America, 1630-1875.* Chicago: University of Chicago Press, 1988. (Most of the quotations in this chapter are drawn from this work.)

Lambert, Byron Cecil. *The Rise of the Anti-Mission Baptists: Sources and Leaders, 1800–1840.* New York: Arno Press, 1980.

Lumpkin, William L. *Baptist Foundations in the South.* Nashville: Broadman Press, 1961.

McLoughlin, William G. *New England Dissent, 1630–1833: The Baptists and the Separation of Church and State.* Cambridge: Harvard University Press, 1971. Volume 1.

Purefoy, George W. *A History of the Sandy Creek Baptist Association, from its Organization in A.D. 1758, to A.D. 1858.* New York: Sheldon & Co., 1859.

Tull, James E. *A History of Southern Baptist Landmarkism in the Light of Historical Baptist Ecclesiology.* New York: Arno Press, 1980.

7/Our Roots in the Age of Reason

"No proposition can be received for divine revelation, or obtain the assent due to all such, if it be contradictory to our clear intuitive knowledge .... Reason must be our last judge and guide in everything."

JOHN LOCKE (1690)

W hile Churches of Christ have firm roots in the Reformed side of the Protestant Reformation, their roots also reach deeply into the eighteenth century Age of Reason, sometimes called the Enlightenment.

What was the Enlightenment, and what is the relation Churches of Christ sustain to that heritage? Answers to these questions form the substance of this chapter.

Religious Wars of the Seventeenth Century

To understand the Enlightenment, one must first grasp the fact that the previous century, the seventeenth, was a century filled with religious wars. Uncounted thousands died in that period simply because they could not agree with the religious perspective of those around them. Most commonly these conflicts pitted Catholics against Protestants, as in the Thirty Years' War on the European continent (1618-1648) and the Catholic persecution of Huguenots (French Calvinists) in France.

Never before in the history of Christendom had believers taken the sword against one another in such wholesale slaughter. During the first three centuries of the Christian faith Christians suffered persecution from a secular state, to be sure. But between 312 and 337 A.D., the Emperor Constantine legalized the Christian faith, and in 380, Theodosius I made Christianity the official faith of the Roman Empire, called on bishops to formulate an orthodox statement of faith (the Council of Constantinople, 381 A.D.), and crushed dissent. From that time until the Protestant Reformation, European Christendom was unified: the popes and the councils defined orthodoxy which in turn was enforced by the state. Consequently, for the next 1,150 years, European Christendom was at relative peace.

But two developments in the sixteenth century changed all that. First was the Protestant Reformation itself, splintering Christendom into numerous rival groups: Lutherans, Zwinglians, Calvinists, Anabaptists, and Anglicans, among others. While these Protestant groups could not agree among themselves, they were at least agreed in their opposition to the Roman Catholic Church which returned their hostility in full measure.

The second development was the translation of Scripture into the vernacular. For well over a thousand years, the Bible had been a closed book, existing only in Latin and accessible only to priests. But in 1526 William Tyndale published the complete New Testament in English, and by 1522 Luther had translated the Bible into German. Suddenly the Bible was an open book. The implications of this development were immense. In this context, it meant the end of religious uniformity for it opened the Bible to individual interpretation.

Differences over interpretation abounded in the sixteenth century, but by the seventeenth century theological positions had hardened and differences erupted into open warfare.

What, then, was the Enlightenment?

Most of all, the Enlightenment began as a response to the religious wars of the seventeenth century and an attempt to end the conflicts. If the wars had been fanned by unbridled emotions, the Enlightenment would focus on reason. Consequently, the eighteenth century is often called the "Age of Reason."

The Rise of Deism

While the Enlightenment flowered in the eighteenth century, its beginnings in England can be traced to 1624 when Lord Herbert of Cherbury wrote a book entitled simply, *De Veritate* (The Truth). A man before his time, Herbert is often called "the Father of the English Enlightenment" and laid the foundations for the religious perspective later called Deism.

Deeply distressed over the Thirty Years' War which then ravaged the Continent, Herbert asked serious questions about religion's role in that war. He well knew that Europe had never been engulfed in religious wars so long as the Roman Church had no rivals and so long as the Bible had been a book closed to private interpretation. Herbert concluded, therefore, that the real source of religious conflict was the Bible itself. After all, it was private interpretation of the Bible that sustained the feuding religious groups.

But Herbert rejoiced that God had not authored one book only, but two books. His second book, Herbert said, was the book of nature which teaches the basics of all religious faiths to all reasonable men and women. Herbert posited that nature clearly teaches the existence of God. To Herbert, nature was a wonderful machine, set in motion by its Maker. What reasonable person, he asked, could observe its regularity, symmetry and efficiency, and fail to conclude that there is a God?

Further, Herbert argued that nature proclaims the existence of a moral order, the reality of right and wrong. All know, for example, that we should not kill or steal or lie, and we know these things by the light of nature. No one needs to read the Bible to discover the moral structure of the universe since that moral structure is self-evident to reasonable human beings.

And further, Herbert said, we can know from observing nature that those who do the right will be rewarded eternally while those who violate the moral code of nature will be punished eternally.

These doctrines so clearly taught by nature, Herbert went on, were the central dogmas of all religions. He therefore advised Europeans to abandon the Bible as the sole source of religious faith and to adopt instead a religion of reason which would find its theology in God's second book, that of nature.

At this point, we must be very clear concerning Herbert's means and ends since, interestingly, Herbert's agenda had an immense impact on the emergence of Churches of Christ in the nineteenth century. Herbert was fundamentally concerned with the pragmatic question of Christian unity. That was his objective and his end. The means he proposed to achieve that goal was this: reduce religion to a set of essentials on which all reasonable people can agree. As it happened, he was convinced that those essentials should be drawn from nature, not from Scripture. But that fact should not obscure his basic concern: reducing religion to bare essentials to provide a platform upon which all reasonable men and women could agree, thus ending wars and schisms and unifying Christendom.

John Locke and the Supernatural Rationalists

If his passion for unity drove Herbert to substitute nature for the Bible, others later in the century agreed with his objectives but questioned his means. These were the Supernatural Rationalists, most eloquently represented by John Locke.

Religious wars and persecutions distressed Locke as they had Herbert before him. He would not, however, exchange the Bible for nature's teachings. At the same time, he knew that insistence on *all* biblical teachings would simply perpetuate religious strife, divisions, persecutions, and perhaps even religious wars.

Locke's solution to the problem was twofold. First, he argued in his famous *Essays on Toleration* that government had no legitimate right to enforce religious orthodoxy. Indeed, religion was no proper sphere of government intervention at all. In making this case, Locke effectively removed the source of religious wars by divorcing religion from the legitimate concerns of the state.

But what might prevent wars and persecutions instigated not by rulers but by the people? Here, Locke adopted Herbert's proposal to reduce religion to a set of essentials upon which all reasonable persons could agree. However—and this is the critical point—he applied that agenda to the Bible. Thus, in his famous book, *The Reasonableness of Christianity*, Locke concluded that Christianity is a reasonable faith, especially in its essentials: the

John Locke: this Enlightenment philosopher looked to human reason as the final test of truth. (Philosophical Library)

Messiahship of Jesus and obedience to his clear commands. All other biblical teachings Locke viewed as non-essential issues which individual Christians might devoutly embrace but over which they should never coerce, fight, or kill.

In this way, Locke rescued the Bible from the oblivion to which it had been relegated by Herbert and the Deists. Further, he even made the Bible—at least in its essentials—the basis for religious unity in Europe.

Beyond this, it is important to mark what Locke did not do. He did not urge obedience to the Bible in all its commands and examples. Nor did he urge restoration of the primitive church in all its details. That had been the Puritan teaching, and Locke agreed with Herbert that the Puritan concept had been largely responsible for the wars and bloodshed in England. Locke, therefore, reduced Christianity to two essentials only: the belief that Jesus Christ is the Messiah, and obedience to all his clear and evident commands.

The Campbell Movement

When Thomas Campbell arrived in America from Ireland in 1807, he found on these shores intense denominational rivalries dividing Christians from one another. Christians were not at war, to be sure, but he saw in American religion the very spirit that had nourished the religious wars and persecutions in Europe years before. The deep divisions among Christians entered his own life when he sought to share communion with Presbyterians in southwest Pennsylvania who did not belong to his rigidly orthodox Presbyterian sect—the Old Light, Anti-Burgher, Seceder Presbyterian Church. For this transgression, the Pittsburgh Synod summarily dismissed Campbell from his preaching appointment.

Campbell now began to meet with sympathetic friends in his neighborhood, seeking a way to unify a badly divided American church. He and his friends organized the Christian Association of Washington which subsequently drew up *The Declaration and Address*, the document that would become the charter statement for the Campbell movement in America. Thomas Campbell was its chief author.

Campbell dealt with the problem of religious division by employing the same philosophy that Herbert of Cherbury and John Locke had employed years before: reduce religion to a set of essentials upon which all reasonable persons might agree. It is true that he specifically avoided the term "essentials," but he clearly employed the concept throughout this important document.

In *The Declaration and Address*, Campbell bewailed religious division and strife.

> . . . tired and sick of the bitter jarrings and janglings of a party spirit, we would desire to be at rest; and, were it possible, we would also desire to adopt and recommend such measures as would give rest to our brethren throughout all the churches: as would restore unity, peace, and purity to the whole Church of God.

Thomas Campbell: chief author of a unity proposal entitled The Declaration and Address. *(courtesy of Bill Humble, Abilene, TX)*

As the solution, he called for Christians to

> reduce to practice that simple original form of Christianity, expressly exhibited upon the sacred page; without attempting to inculcate anything of human authority, of private opinion, or inventions of men, as having any place in the constitution, faith, or worship, of the Christian Church, or anything as a matter of Christian faith or duty, for which there can not be expressly produced a "Thus saith the Lord," either in express terms or by approved precedent.

What then were those essentials upon which all reasonable persons might agree? Only those practices for which there was in Scripture a clear "'Thus saith the Lord,' either in express terms, or by approved precedent."

We should not be surprised that Campbell would adopt such a formula for unity. After all, he was chronologically a child of the eighteenth-century Enlightenment, having been born in 1763. But more than this, he was a diligent student of Enlightenment thought and especially of John Locke, and was well acquainted with the tradition of reducing religion to essentials upon which all reasonable persons might agree. Thus, when faced with religious strife and division in America, he naturally employed this tradition which he knew so well.

Still, there was a radical difference between Thomas Campbell on the one hand, and Herbert and Locke on the other. In his search for religious unity, Herbert had expelled the Bible in favor of the plain and simple teachings of nature. Locke then rescued the Bible but limited its essentials only to the theme that Jesus is the Messiah and should be obeyed in all his explicit commands. For both Herbert and Locke, the old Puritan agenda of restoring primitive Christianity was inherently divisive and should be avoided at all costs. Campbell, however, in *The Declaration and Address*, identified the essentials of the Christian faith as consisting of whatever God commanded, "either in express terms, or by approved precedent." He argued that the essentials of the Christian faith required a complete restoration of apostolic Christianity. Thus, he asked in *The Declaration and Address*,

> Were we, then, in our Church constitution and managements, to exhibit a complete conformity to the apostolic Church, would we not be, in that respect, as perfect as Christ intended we should be?

It is clear, then, that Campbell merged the restoration philosophy he had inherited from the Reformed and Puritan traditions with the Enlightenment approach he had inherited from the Age of Reason. This bonding of Puritan and Enlightenment thought would cause serious problems for Churches of Christ in the years to come. But this is a story we will tell in chapter nine.

A Rational Christianity

A rational formula for unity was not the only contribution the Enlightenment made to Churches of Christ. Beyond this, the Enlightenment infused our movement with a rational perspective according to which the Bible itself became a sort of scientific manual, a constitution, or a technical blueprint.

It is essential to appreciate at this point the absolute triumph of reason, science, and a scientific worldview in the eighteenth century. Two factors produced this triumph.

In the first place, Europeans turned to scientific rationalism in reaction against the "enthusiasm" of the religious wars. Alexander Pope (1688–1744) caught the spirit of the age when he wrote, "For modes of faith, let graceless zealots fight." Instead of fighting, rational demonstration of the truth of one's position would win the day.

In the second place, the principles of science and the scientific method were making deep inroads into European civilization by the eighteenth century. In the previous century, the scientific writings of Isaac Newton (1642–1727) popularized the perspective that the universe was ruled not by the arbitrary will of deity but by the natural laws of cause and effect. Somewhat earlier, Rene' Descartes (1596–1650) had argued that all mental conceptions should be doubted until adequately proven, and that proof, to be adequate, must have the certainty of mathematics. Between them, Newton and Descartes made popular a perspective that glorified reason, not religion. And that perspective blossomed into full flower by the eighteenth century.

Given the prevalence of this viewpoint by 1700, many believers concluded that if Christianity was to be viable for their age, it must be cast in a scientific mold and must rest on a rational foundation. Thus a host of Europeans—both Deists and Supernatural Rationalists—rushed to show that Christianity was fundamentally compatible with a rational, scientific worldview. Popular treatises appeared in England with titles like *Christianity Not Mysterious* (John Toland, 1696) or *Christianity as Old as Creation* (Mathew Tindal, 1730). These books sought to show that Christianity was rational and fundamentally in harmony with the laws of nature and science.

Hosts of eighteenth-century believers adopted this perspective. After all, it seemed clear to them that their contemporaries would not take seriously any defense of the Christian faith not rooted in a rational and scientific worldview.

In reaching this conclusion, they made an important concession to the spirit of their age. In effect, they conceded that neither the authority of the Bible nor the authority of God were adequate to legitimate the Christian faith. Indeed, the final court of appeal was reason. Thus the teachings of the Bible, so long as they were reasonable, were legitimate. But the clear implication, sometimes boldly stated, was that the Bible's teachings might be abandoned altogether if found unreasonable.

Once committed to this position, it was inevitable that Christians increasingly would defend the Bible as a scientific document as skeptics increasingly attacked its doctrines as unreasonable. And in the process, believers increasingly treated the Bible as a book of rational facts, comparable to any other scientific text.

In Scotland, this perspective reached its zenith in the school of Common Sense Realism led by Thomas Reid (1710–1796) and Dugald Stewart (1753–1828). These men taught that the Bible should be treated as a compendium of concrete facts, not as a book of abstract truths. Further, proper interpretation of the Bible must begin with facts. The theologian's task was to search out from the Bible all the facts pertinent to a given topic, arrange those facts in order, and then finally draw conclusions. This of course was nothing less than the scientific method applied to the Bible.

Since the Common Sense school, therefore, invoked the scientific method as the only proper method of biblical interpretation, it was often labeled "Baconianism" after Sir Francis Bacon, founder of the scientific method.

Rational Christianity Among Churches of Christ

What is important for Churches of Christ is this: Alexander Campbell, Thomas Campbell's son and the most influential leader of Churches of Christ in the nineteenth century, was deeply devoted to the Common Sense perspective. Campbell argued over and again that "the Bible is a book of facts, not of opinions, theories, abstract generalities, nor of verbal definitions."

Baconianism appealed to Campbell especially because it promised a sure foundation for Christian unity. After all, when scientists confined themselves to facts, agreement prevailed. In the same way, Campbell supposed, agreement must prevail among Christians who simply confine themselves to the facts of "this divine science of religion."

Campbell not only advised his people to confine themselves to biblical "facts." He also advised them to confine themselves to biblical words, since adherence to biblical words was the surest way to adhere to biblical "facts." After all, if Christians would, as Campbell put it, "abandon every word and sentence not found in the Bible" and would use instead only scriptural language when discussing biblical issues, disagreements and divisions would be virtually impossible.

Clearly, the eighteenth-century Enlightenment had profoundly shaped Campbell's understanding of the Bible. For Campbell, the Bible was a book of theological truths, to be sure, but even more it was a collection of facts that should be scientifically and rationally understood—facts that collectively comprised a kind of blueprint or constitution.

What frightened Campbell most in this regard was the supposition, so common in his time, that the Holy Spirit might work on the hearts of men and women separate and apart from the Bible. Campbell rightly surmised that such a view undermined a rational and scientific approach to the biblical text. After all, while a scientific, factual Bible was both manageable and predictable, a Spirit who moved freely in the hearts and minds of Christians would be neither.

While Campbell therefore refused to confine the Spirit to the biblical text altogether, many of his statements tended in that direction. Thus he wrote in 1824, "Since those gifts [of the Spirit] have ceased, the Holy Spirit now operates upon the minds of men only by the word." He even argued that "if the Spirit of God has spoken all its arguments" in Scripture, then "all the power of the Holy Spirit which can operate on the human mind is spent."

In time such a position became orthodoxy among Churches of Christ. B. F. Hall perhaps typified most when he wrote in 1837,

> ... I believe that the Holy Spirit exerts no influence on the heart of sinners over and above the word: that his influences are in the facts he has revealed in the gospel, the evidence by which he has confirmed these facts, and in the motives to obedience presented in the Scriptures of Truth.

Thus, long before the Civil War, a thoroughly rational understanding of the Christian faith prevailed among Churches of Christ.

Conclusion

The eighteenth-century Enlightenment, then, shaped Churches of Christ in two fundamental respects.

First, the Enlightenment taught our fathers that the surest way to Christian union was to reduce religion to a set of essentials upon which all reasonable persons could agree. And for our fathers, those essentials were found in the outlines of the primitive church. Second, the Enlightenment taught our fathers the importance of a rational faith, rationally formulated, rationally defended, and predicated on the "facts" of a rational Bible.

To these perspectives of the eighteenth-century Enlightenment, Churches of Christ are heir.

Questions

1. To what aspect of the seventeenth century was the Enlightenment a reaction? What were the ultimate goals and objectives both of Lord Herbert of Cherbury and of John Locke?

2. In what ways did John Locke differ from Herbert of Cherbury?

3. How did Thomas Campbell adopt and apply the perspectives of Herbert and Locke? In what important ways did Campbell differ from Herbert and Locke?

4. Why did believers in the eighteenth century think it so important to defend the Bible as a rational and scientific book? In what ways did they actually damage the Bible's credibility in adopting this defense?

5. How did the Scottish school of Common Sense render the Bible essentially a rational, scientific text? Why?

6. Why did Alexander Campbell find the Common Sense perspective so appealing?

7. What did Campbell's adoption of the Common Sense perspective mean for Churches of Christ? For our view of the Bible? For our understanding of the Holy Spirit?

8. Would you assess the impact of the Enlightenment on Churches of Christ in positive or negative terms? Why? If negative, explain what a better perspective might be?

For Further Study

*Allen, C. Leonard. "Baconianism and the Bible in the Disciples of Christ: James S. Lamar and *The Organon of Scripture.*" *Church History* 55 (March 1986):65–80.

Bozeman, T. Dwight. *Protestants in an Age of Science: The Baconian Ideal in Antebellum American Religious Thought.* Chapel Hill, NC: University of North Carolina Press, 1977.

Cragg, Gerald R. *From Puritanism to the Age of Reason.* Cambridge, England: Cambridge University Press, 1950.

May, Henry F. *The Enlightenment in America.* New York: Oxford University Press, 1976.

*Turner, James. "Enlightenment and Belief, 1600–1750." In *Without God, Without Creed: The Rise of Unbelief in America.* Baltimore: Johns Hopkins University Press, 1985.

8/Our Roots in the American Experience

"When we shall have unlearned everything which has been taught since his [Jesus'] day, and got back to the pure and simple doctrines he inculcated, we shall then be truly and worthily his disciples; and my opinion is that if nothing had ever been added to what flowed purely from his lips, the whole world would at this day have been Christian."

THOMAS JEFFERSON (1821)

In America, especially following the Revolution of 1776, the restoration sentiment blossomed as perhaps never before. Many thousands turned their backs on traditional religion and sought to recover the primitive church. The heady ideal of primitive Christianity became compelling and even irresistible in those halcyon days, particularly in the West.

The restoration sentiment in those years wore many faces. Those who turned to "primitive Christianity" often differed dramatically from one another, both in their view of the Bible and in their understanding of what apostolic Christianity was all about.

The wide variety of restorationists in the new nation becomes apparent when we realize that alongside Churches of Christ were Baptists, Mormons, Shakers, and other radical sects who intended to restore primitive Christianity and viewed that task as central to their work.

This chapter proposes several reasons for the immense popularity of the restoration ideal on the nineteenth-century American frontier. To underscore the diversity of restoration movements in those years, we focus in this chapter on one tradition that was self-consciously restorationist, yet radically dissimilar to Churches of Christ: the Mormons. An understanding of the Mormon restoration in the context of its time aids comprehension of how that same context might have shaped the restoration movement which produced the Churches of Christ.

Failure to understand the cultural milieu that sustained Mormons in their quest for the primitive faith will shroud the very context of life that shaped our identity and sustained our growth in the early years.

Popularity of the Restoration Ideal

At least five factors helped make the restoration sentiment immensely appealing in the early years of American nationhood.

First, the American land itself seemed uncorrupted and undefiled. To many immigrants from European cities whose streets were fouled with garbage, whose air was polluted, and whose corridors were congested with civilization, America seemed like Eden itself. If the European world had once been pure, fresh from the creative hands of God, it now was defiled almost everywhere by "progress" and civilization.

Yet Eden remained in America—or so it seemed to countless immigrants in the early nineteenth century. Such a land, pristine and undefiled by human impositions, seemed the perfect place to recover pure, uncorrupted, and original Christianity. At the same time, the old European churches—so laden with customs, traditions, and human decrees—seemed strangely out of place in this American Eden. For many newcomers to America, therefore, only one religious option made sense: to restore the faith, life, and structure of the Christian religion when it was fresh, pure, and new.

Second, in the eyes of many at the time, the American experiment in democracy appeared to be just the sort of government God intended when he first created the heavens and the earth. The government, then, seemed as fresh and pure as the land itself. Thomas Paine, friend of Thomas Jefferson, perhaps put it best when he proclaimed that the American government was like "the beginning of a world . . . . We are brought at once to the point of seeing government begin, as if we had lived in the beginning of time . . . , unmutilated by contrivance, or the errors of tradition."

Paine's phrase, "the unmutilated beginning of time," described America for many in the nation. This meant that the Founding Fathers had themselves been agents of restoration. The question that nagged at many Christians, therefore, was this: if the Founders had restored the God-intended form of government, could Christians do any less with the church? Was it not incumbent on Christians to abandon the traditions and customs that had grown up over centuries of Christian history and to return to the wellsprings of the Christian faith?

Third, America's edenic qualities led many to suppose that this nation would launch the millennial dawn. For centuries, many had dreamed of a millennial age of justice, righteousness, and peace on earth. But that age had not arrived. Instead, Europeans suffered tyrannies and repressions. The freedom to worship, speak, and write according to one's convictions typically was unthinkable.

Now, however, in this new land, a marvelous constitution had provided for representative government and had guaranteed freedoms that simply boggled the minds of many immigrants. The millennium, many thought, must surely be at hand.

Even today this millennial anticipation finds graphic expression on the Great Seal of the United States reproduced on the one-dollar bill. On the seal an unfinished pyramid with 1776 at its base rises from the sands of an arid desert floor. The desert implicitly suggests the human past before 1776. But in 1776, something new, fresh, and pure emerged from the desert sands, and that something was America. Above the pyramid the eye of God surveys the scene and God himself pronounces his approval: *annuit coeptis*, or, "He has smiled on our beginnings." Beneath the pyramid stands the telling phrase, *novus ordo seclorum*, or, "A new order of the ages."

And so it seemed. America was a new order of the ages, unlike any nation in all the human past. Further, America was new precisely because it had restored the old. If time-worn traditions enmeshed other nations, America had restored the way things were meant to be when the world was new.

The pyramid on the Great Seal, however, is incomplete, signifying that the widely expected golden age lies still in the future. Through the power of example, however, America would lead other nations in the paths of first times. Then, when freedom and democracy had encompassed the globe, the pyramid would be complete and the millennial age would have dawned.

The Great Seal of the United States: proclaiming "A New Order of the Ages."

In all of this, the nation provided Christians with a highly instructive example. The nation had restored first times. Why had not the church? Further, was it not the rightful task of the church to build the millennial kingdom? Should not the church also commit itself to restore first times and to hasten the millennial age? Countless American Christians, therefore, rushed to discover the pattern of the primitive church, to rebuild that church in the new American nation, and thereby to hasten the millennial age.

A fourth reason for the immense popularity of the restoration ideal in the early nineteenth century was its promise of independence from the older, European churches. The American Revolution had liberated Americans from political bondage, yet many still felt bound by time-worn traditions enforced by clerics and creeds. Because these traditions were rooted in centuries of history, the surest way of escape lay in declaring church history itself irrelevant.

Thousands of American Christians, therefore, renounced Christian history altogether and claimed to recognize no jurisdiction whatever except the Bible and the primitive church. In this way, individual Christians freed themselves to interpret the Bible on their own, totally apart from the "orthodoxy" which any particular denomination might wish to promote through its clerics and its creeds.

Finally the idea of primitive faith appealed to many because it promised the assurance of being right amid the welter of claims and counter-claims of the competing denominations. For Christians in twentieth-century America, it may be difficult to grasp the significance of this appeal, but for Christians in 1800, it held great power indeed. Those who came to America from Europe had been accustomed to only one church, and that one church was officially established by law. All other churches were illegal. It would never have occurred to most Europeans to ask, "Which of all the churches is the true church?" There was but one.

In America, however, the situation was different. Churches from all parts of Europe took root on these shores, and by 1800 numerous denominations competed for the allegiance of American citizens. Baptists, Congregationalists, Lutherans, Presbyterians, Methodists, Episcopalians, Quakers, Roman Catholics and numerous smaller groups each claimed God's truth. One can imagine the distress this American situation might cause for someone whose native land had only one church.

Rather than sort through the competing denominational claims to learn which one was right and which wrong, many Americans dismissed the claims altogether and turned directly to the Bible. They thought that by taking their stand firmly on the Bible and the primitive church, they could be assured that they were right regardless of the claims of the churches. In this way, the fact of religious pluralism itself provided a powerful incentive to search Scripture for the true form of the primitive church.

A return to primitive Christianity was thus a powerful and appealing idea in the new American nation. It was an old idea with which most people with Puritan or Reformed Protestant roots were likely to have some acquaintance. Then, in the newness of the American land and the American nation, the appeal to first times took root in remarkably fertile soil. This appeal served at least three purposes: it seemed the perfect foundation on which to build the millennial kingdom; it seemed the ideal antidote to the tyrannies of creeds and clerics; and it promised assurance of being right amid the claims and counter-claims of warring sects.

The Mormons

No group used the language of "restoration" more consistently and more effectively than did the Church of Jesus Christ of Latter-day Saints or the Mormons.

Vast differences obviously exist between the Latter-day Saints and the Churches of Christ, not the least of which is the Book of Mormon. But these differences should not obscure the fact that early Mormons seemed obsessed with restoring the ancient church of God. Early Mormons envisioned restoration in ways quite foreign to members of Churches of Christ, but their commitment to the restoration principle was as unrelenting as that of any of the early leaders of our own restoration movement.

The touchstone for Mormon restoration ideas was Acts 3:20–21 (KJV): "And he shall send Jesus Christ, which before was preached unto you: whom the heaven must receive until the times of restitution [restoration] of all things, which God hath spoken by the mouth of all his holy prophets since the world began." Drawing upon this text, early Mormons spoke constantly of "the restoration of all things," and took that phrase as descriptive of what their church was all about.

Joseph Smith described the Latter-day Saints as "engaged in the very same order of things as observed by the holy Apostles of old . . . ." He preached that "the God of heaven has begun to restore the ancient order of His kingdom unto His servants and His people," and he proclaimed that the people involved in that great work were the Latter-day Saints.

Even today Mormons continue to employ the language of restoration and argue that the ancient church of God disappeared following its early days and was restored to the earth by the Prophet Joseph Smith on April 6, 1830. Even modern, authorized histories of the Latter-day Saints sometimes bear such titles as *Joseph Smith and the Restoration*.

Some members of Churches of Christ, aware of the restorationist dimensions of the Latter-day Saints, have claimed that Mormonism might never have taken the form it did had it not been for an apostate preacher in the Campbell movement, Sidney Rigdon. Rigdon led a congregation aligned with the Campbell movement in Kirtland, Ohio, into the Mormon fold and later became close friends with Joseph Smith. Many argue that Sidney Rigdon taught Smith restoration philosophy. Yet given the pervasive appeal of the restoration idea in the early nineteenth century, it is likely that Mormonism would have adopted restoration principles regardless of any influence from either Sidney Rigdon or Alexander Campbell.

Churches of Christ cannot take credit either for inventing or popularizing the restoration idea in those years. Mormons and Churches of Christ both represent diverse expressions of a popular theme that had long existed independently of either group. Just as Alexander Campbell inherited the restoration principle from a variety of sources, so also did Joseph Smith and his Mormon colleagues. Mormonism is especially intriguing, however, since its history and theology reflect, in one way or another, practically all the cultural currents discussed in the previous section which rendered the restoration ideal so appealing in early nineteenth-century America.

Mormonism and American Culture

Part of the appeal of the restoration theme was the assurance it provided that one was right. This concern for correctness amid a welter of competing faiths provided the chief impulse behind the birth of Mormonism.

According to Joseph's recollections, the wide assortment of religious denominations competing in the free market of souls in upstate New York had caused him no small amount of consternation. Smith therefore asked the Lord which of all the churches is the true church? The answer was that "they were all wrong," and that "all their creeds were an abomination in His sight." For the next several years, Joseph, like Roger Williams two hundred years before, became a seeker, waiting for the restoration of true Christianity.

The Book of Mormon, purportedly translated from secret golden plates by Joseph Smith, was a central part of the Mormon restoration. This sample of the writing on the plates was drawn by one who claimed to have seen them.

But while Williams died a seeker, waiting for the prophet who would restore the ancient faith, Smith thought himself the very prophet through whom the restoration would occur.

Smith's restoration began in 1827 when he unearthed his golden plates—the basis for the *Book of Mormon*—near his home in upstate New York, and on April 6, 1830, he officially organized the "Church of Christ." To distinguish this new church from other "churches of Christ," however, Smith later changed the name to the "Church of Jesus Christ of Latter-day Saints."

For Smith and his Mormon colleagues restoration meant something very different from what it meant for Barton Stone, Alexander Campbell, and heirs of the Stone-Campbell movement today. Neither rationalism nor forms and structures were central to the task of restoration. Restoration meant, above all, recovering direct communion and conversation with God himself as in biblical days. Since the apostasy had closed the heavens and stilled direct communion between God and humankind, so the first objective of the Mormon restoration was to revive direct communion with the Spirit of God. This was the heart of their restoration effort.

This passion to experience again the Spirit of God led Mormons to live for a while on the site of what they believed was the Garden of Eden (Davies County, Missouri). They established a Church of Jesus Christ which, under an Aaronic priesthood, practiced in a restored "Jewish" temple the ancient Christian rite of baptism for the remission of sins, and even introduced the ancient patriarchal practice of polygamy. Through it all, Mormons claimed to experience the Spirit of God, not just to restore the forms and structures of ancient days.

Mormonism also tapped a deep interest in millennialism that was so prevalent in America in the early nineteenth century. The very name, Church of Jesus Christ of Latter-day Saints, reflects the Mormon interest in both first times and last times. "Church of Jesus Christ" meant for Mormons that this was no ordinary church, born of history and tradition. Rather, this was the restored church, the one and only Church of Jesus Christ. "Latter-day Saints" revealed the Mormon belief that the last days were at hand when Jesus would soon return to earth, gather the Latter-day Saints to himself, and rule the earth both from Jerusalem and from the Mormon Zion, Jackson County, Missouri.

Another theme central for Mormons was America's strategic role in God's plan. The *Book of Mormon* tells how Christ came to the Americas to preach shortly after completing his Palestinian ministry. If the Bible, therefore, records God's dealings with the Old World, the Book of Mormon records his dealings with the New.

In Mormon thinking, America played a strategic role in the kingdom of God. The Garden of Eden lay in the great American heartland, Jesus himself preached in America, and Jesus would return to rule the earth for one thousand years from an American Zion. In its celebration of America, Mormon theology expressed commonly cherished convictions about the meaning of America in that age. This fact alone goes far to explain Mormonism's immense appeal both then and now.

What Have We Learned?

While the Latter-day Saints form no part of the ancestry of the Stone-Campbell movement, Mormonism demonstrates as does no other religion the close connection between American culture in the early nineteenth century and the popularity of the restoration sentiment.

Were Americans perplexed by the diversity of religions, all competing in the same free market of souls? Mormonism answered: they are all wrong, and only the restored Church of Jesus Christ is true and right.

Did Americans seek to be free from the tyranny of creeds and clerics? Mormonism answered: it is possible to bypass creeds and clerics and commune directly with the Spirit of God in the restored Church of Christ.

Did Americans view their nation as a new order of the ages which would launch the millennial dawn? Mormonism answered: the true, restored Church of Jesus Christ of Latter-day Saints would hasten the millenial age, and its members would reign with Christ for a thousand years.

Did Americans view both their land and their government as essentially edenic, partaking of the first age before the fall? Mormonism answered: the church in this land must also be born of first times, and that is precisely the church that Joseph Smith claimed to have restored on April 6, 1830.

One's own views can sometimes be better understood against the backdrop of others who hold important perspectives in common. Members of Churches of Christ may see in Mormonism the close relation between the restoration ideal and early American culture. Against that backdrop, might we now discern similar connections between ourselves and the culture that nourished our movement in the early nineteenth century?

We will attempt to discover those links as we turn next to the birth of our own movement in that same age.

Questions

1. Explain five ways in which American culture in the early nineteenth century encouraged the growth and popularity of the restoration ideal.

2. What convictions did Churches of Christ and Latter-day Saints share in common during the early nineteenth century in America?

3. How did early Mormonism respond to the reality of religious pluralism in America?

4. What role did America itself play in Mormon thought?

5. What aspect of early Christian life and experience did Mormons principally seek to recover?

6. What chief difference(s) do you see between the goal of restoration as conceived by Churches of Christ and the goal of restoration as conceived by Mormons?

7. If we understand something about the culture and circumstances in which American Churches of Christ first took root and began to grow, how might that help us understand ourselves today?

8. What might we learn about ourselves by studying the restoration plea as embraced by early Mormons?

For Further Study

American Backgrounds

Gaustad, Edwin S. "Restitution, Revolution, and the American Dream." *Journal of the American Academy of Religion* 44 (March 1976): 77-86

Hill, Samuel S. "A Typology of American Restitutionism: From Frontier Revivalism and Mormonism to the Jesus Movement." *Journal of the American Academy of Religion* 44 (March 1976):65–76.

*Hatch, Nathan O. "*Sola Scriptura* and *Novus Ordo Seclorum*." In *The Bible in America: Essays in Cultural History*. Edited by Nathan Hatch and Mark Noll. New York: Oxford University Press, 1982.

Mead, Sidney E. "Denominationalism: The Shape of Protestantism in America." In *The Lively Experiment*. New York: Harper and Row, 1963.

Mormons

Arrington, Leonard and Bitton, Davis. *The Mormon Experience: A History of the Latter-day Saints*. New York: Alfred Knopf, 1979.

Barrett, Ivan. *Joseph Smith and the Restoration: A History of the Church to 1846*. Provo, Utah: Young House and Brigham Young University Press, 1973.

Bushman, Richard. *Joseph Smith and the Beginnings of Mormonism*. Urbana: University of Illinois Press, 1985.

*Hughes, Richard T. "Soaring With the Gods: Early Mormonism and the Eclipse of Religious Pluralism." In *The Lively Experiment Continued*. Edited by Jerald C. Brauer. Macon, GA: Mercer University Press, 1987.

Petersen, Mark E. *The Great Prologue.* Salt Lake City: Deseret Book Company, 1975. (Explains the relation of Latter-day Saints to America and American institutions.)

Shipps, Jan. *Mormonism: The Story of a New Religious Tradition.* Urbana: University of Illinois Press, 1986.

9/The Birth of Our Movement

"The religion of Heaven, for centuries past, has fallen far below the excellency and glory of primitive Christianity. [We seek] to have these errors corrected and removed from the church; and to have truth restored in her heavenly, captivating robes, unadorned with the tinsel of human wisdom."

BARTON W. STONE (1826)

When American Churches of Christ emerged in the early nineteenth century, they inherited many of the factors we have discussed to this point: a long tradition of restoration thinking reaching back to the sixteenth-century Reformation; an edenic landscape in a "natural" nation that encouraged a return to first times; anticipation of an imminent millennium; perplexity over religious pluralism; and perhaps most important a deep commitment to political and religious freedom.

All these factors encouraged Americans to take the Bible and the Bible alone as their only guide to Christian faith and practice.

Early Stirrings

Perhaps the single most striking aspect of our movement's early years was its simultaneous emergence in four widely separate locales under four different leaders, each initially unaware of the work of the others. The work and following of two of these leaders—James O'Kelly and Elias Smith—were not critical to the later institutional development of Churches of Christ but still deserve mention here.

James O'Kelly, a man passionately dedicated to freedom, led the first of these movements which centered in Virginia and North Carolina. A Methodist circuit rider, O'Kelly chafed under the clerical authority of Bishop Francis Asbury who, O'Kelly felt, ruled the Methodist Church in arbitrary and even tyrannical ways. O'Kelly and several other Methodist ministers, therefore, withdrew from the Methodists in 1792 and constituted themselves "Republican Methodists." Two years later, Rice Haggard convinced these dissenters that they should reject all names born of history and tradition and call themselves simply "Christians."

During the same period, a similar movement emerged in New England under the leadership of Abner Jones and, even more important, Elias Smith. A radical Jeffersonian, Smith resisted every encroachment on his liberty, perceived or real, that emanated from the established churches, and dedicated himself to shearing those churches of their power. Coming from a Separate Baptist background and therefore well-acquainted with the rhetoric of restorationism, Smith insisted on the recovery of a primitive church in which members would be simply Christians and over which human traditions would hold no sway. He attracted a significant following and the heirs of O'Kelly and Smith later joined ranks to form the Christian Connection. The movement ultimately merged into the United Church of Christ, a contemporary denomination that also has deep roots in the Puritan movement.

Barton W. Stone

Far more important than either the Smith or O'Kelly movements for later Churches of Christ was another "Christian" movement originating in Kentucky under the leadership of Barton W. Stone. Once again, power and freedom were central issues.

Stone and four other Presbyterian ministers had participated in the highly ecumenical Cane Ridge Revival of 1801. Involved in the revival's charismatic exercises, they had set themselves against the Calvinistic notion of rigid predestination. When one of their number was consequently censured by the Synod of Kentucky for doctrinal deviance, Stone and his colleagues withdrew from the Synod in 1803 and formed their own Springfield Presbytery. Within a year, however, they dissolved that Presbytery and

Barton W. Stone: an early leader of Churches of Christ who focused restoration on holy living and separation from the world. (courtesy of Bill Humble, Abilene, TX)

determined—again, at the urging of Rice Haggard—to become "Christians only."

The Stone movement prospered, especially in Kentucky, Tennessee, northern Alabama, and southern Ohio, and made converts especially among Separate Baptists who already shared a restorationist orientation. By 1811, according to one contemporary source, the Stone movement boasted already some 13,000 adherents. The Stone movement was restorationist, to be sure, but it focused more in its early years on holy and righteous living than on the forms and structures of the primitive church. Restoration for Stone and his colleagues meant first of all restoring the life style of the first Christian communities.

Separation from the world, therefore, was a central theme among the early Stoneite Christians. In the very first issue of Stone's *Christian Messenger* (November 25, 1826), Stone called for "the restoration and glory of the ancient religion of Christ." He defined this concept as walking in the spirit instead of the flesh, as dying to sin and living to God, and as abandoning wealth, pride, and valued relationships for the sake of truth. In this context, Stone and his colleagues rejected slavery, urged compassion for the poor and the downtrodden, and called for separation from the "God-robbing practices" of this world.

While extolling ethics and holy living, the Stone movement also advanced restoration of the primitive church. Their concern for restoration, however, amounted far more to a rejection of historic traditions than to a positive reconstruction of primitive Christian practices. They simply feared that to insist too strongly on particular practices would undermine their newly won freedom.

Baptists, Methodists, and Presbyterians in Virginia and Kentucky had been exceedingly zealous for civic liberty during the revolutionary period. But when the War was over, the tyranny of the clergy persisted, a tyranny that Stone and his colleagues thought particularly apparent in their treatment at the hands of the Synod of Kentucky. Richard McNemar, one of Stone's earliest colleagues, wrote of the Stone movement in its earliest years that "it is difficult to paint the zeal for liberty, and just indignation against the old aristocratic spirit, which glowed through every member of this new confederacy."

In fact, if any one theme was foundational for the Stone movement it was the ideal of freedom. From that foundation, these radicals rejected all the encumbrances of history embodied in creeds, clerics, and tradition, and even jettisoned theology itself. As one of Stone's colleagues observed, "We are not personally acquainted with the writings of John Calvan [sic], nor are we certain how nearly we agree with his views of divine truth; neither do we care." Their gaze was fixed, instead, squarely on primitive Christianity revealed in Holy Writ.

With so strong a commitment to freedom, they avoided developing ecclesiastical traditions of any kind, even those predicated on primitive Christianity. Even believer's baptism, acknowledged by practically all Stoneites as apostolic, was simply left to the discretion of the individual. Consequently, the Stone movement was, from the outset, largely without dogma, form, or structure. The common thread that held the movement together was a commitment to primitive Christianity whose most important features, the Stoneites thought, were Christian character and Christian freedom.

Stoneite primitivism equally stressed the hastening of the millennial kingdom of God. Like so many other Americans of their time, the Stoneites were convinced that the millennium was near. But while most Americans pinned their millennial hopes on the new nation, the Stoneites argued that no mere nation could hasten the kingdom of God. Nor could the churches of history and tradition perform that task. Only the primitive church which stood prior to human traditions could finally hasten the glorious millennial age. In this conviction, the Stoneites were remarkably similar to the Latter-day Saints.

The possibility of an imminent millennium led to another major theme in the Stoneite movement: a demand for Christian unity predicated upon apostolic Christianity. Clearly, a Christendom divided by human traditions could never inaugurate the perfections of the millennial dawn. Stone and his colleagues therefore advocated a restoration of primitive Christianity as a means to Christian unity which in turn would hasten the millennial age.

Precisely at this point the Stoneites dealt with the persistent problem of religious pluralism which so bedeviled Joseph Smith and later James Graves. While admitting the presence of Christians in all Protestant denominations, Stone's followers argued that the denominational structures themselves constituted a Babylonian wilderness of strife and confusion. Therefore, they called upon "Christians in the sects" to "come out of Babylon" and to unite upon the one apostolic foundation. When this task was accomplished, the denominational structures of history would fall, the primitive church would embrace all Christians worldwide, and the millennium would have begun.

Again, Stone and his colleagues understood the task of restoration more as negation of tradition than as creation of new traditions, even apostolic ones. Consequently, the unity for which Stone pled was a unity in freedom rather than a unity in conformity. Freedom, when all was said and done, was the cornerstone of the Stone movement.

Alexander Campbell

The fourth "Christian" movement was that of Thomas and Alexander Campbell. Belonging to the Old Light, Anti-Burgher, Seceder Presbyterian Church in his homeland of Ireland, father Thomas arrived in America in 1807, settled in southwest Pennsylvania, and began preaching under the direction of his church. For sharing communion with Presbyterians of other stripes, however, he was disbarred from his ministry and subsequently withdrew from the Seceder fellowship.

Campbell and several kindred spirits then formed a study group, the Christian Association of Washington, which produced their movement's charter, *The Declaration and Address*. This document articulated the chief preoccupation of the Campbell tradition: Christian unity. But how could unity be achieved? Drawing on the Puritan tradition to which he was heir, Campbell proposed what to him was the obvious solution: recover the common denominator of all Christians—the primitive Christianity reflected in Scripture—and forsake the creeds and traditions of Christian history which had been responsible for maintaining division.

To Campbell the task was clear: the restoration of primitive Christianity would be the means of achieving Christian unity. In this way, father Thomas blended the biblicism of the Puritans with the ecumenical sentiments of the Enlightenment as we indicated in chapter seven.

Thomas' son, Alexander, arrived in America with the remainder of the family in 1809 and quickly assumed leadership of the new movement. The chief instrument of his leadership from 1823 to 1830 was the journal he edited, *The Christian Baptist*.

A student of both John Locke and Common Sense philosophy at Glasgow, Campbell addressed in his paper what he viewed as the heart of the matter: the rational and systematic reconstruction of the apostolic communities. Such restoration, Campbell thought, should entail a clear distinction between the essentials and the non-essentials of primitive Christianity. Thus Campbell rejected the holy kiss, deaconesses, communal living, footwashing, and charismatic exercises as non-essential, and argued for congregational autonomy, a plurality of elders in each congregation, weekly communion, and immersion for the remission of sins as characteristics of the apostolic faith. In this systematic and

Alexander Campbell: the most important single leader of the Restoration Movement who focused on the forms and structures of the primitive church. (courtesy of Bill Humble)

rational reconstruction, Campbell stood in contrast to Barton W. Stone.

While Campbell's movement spread throughout the western reserve, it was singularly successful in Kentucky, Tennessee, and southern Ohio where hearts had been prepared for many years by the work of Barton Stone. In 1823, Campbell made his first trip into the Stone-dominated region of Kentucky in order to debate the Presbyterian W. L. McCalla on the subject of baptism. As a result of that debate and through the circulation of *The Christian Baptist* in Kentucky, Campbell quickly captured the attention of thousands of Stone-Christians who, according to reports of the time, were still unsettled by the radical freedom and the lack of dogma in the Stone movement. For a people already committed to primitive Christianity in principle, Campbell provided form, structure, and a clear, rational definition of primitive Christianity in practice.

The cornerstone of Campbell's rational and systematic portrait of primitive Christianity was his insistence that baptism was immersion and that immersion was for the forgiveness of sins. To Kentucky Calvinists and Stoneites, many uncertain of their election, this notion offered compelling assurance and certainty.

Thus, when the Stoneite preacher B. F. Hall learned this doctrine from a printed copy of the Campbell-McCalla debate in 1826, he was ecstatic. He exulted that he had found "the long lost link in the chain of gospel obedience. . . . I now saw the evidence of remission, which I had never seen before." And John Rogers, another Kentucky Stoneite turned Campbellite, hailed certainty of salvation as itself a mark of the primitive faith. The early Christians, he said, were immersed and were therefore "pardoned, & knew it, & rejoiced in it . . . & never spoke in the language of doubt or fear upon the subject."

By providing structure, order, and certainty, Campbell quickly overshadowed Stone and became the undisputed leader of the "restoration movement," even in the upper South.

In responding to the culture around them, the Campbell and Stone movements agreed at many critical points. Campbell was fully as convinced as Stone that through recovery of primitive Christianity the millennium would dawn. Further, the restoration ideal for Campbell, as for Stone, was a means of winning Christian freedom and shearing the clergy of their power. In addition, the Campbell movement, like Stone's, was a response to religious pluralism, calling for the unity of believers based on an apostolic model.

Tradition Among Churches of Christ

It was over the issue of pluralism, however, that the Campbell movement finally faltered and even divided.

If Campbell's solution to pluralism had been unity through restoration, by the 1840s that platform already was breaking apart. As if to signal that development, Campbell himself discontinued his *Christian Baptist* and launched a more conciliatory journal, *The Millennial Harbinger*, in 1830. As the years passed,

Campbell and his followers in the upper Midwest increasingly accepted unity in pluralistic diversity and subtly downplayed a strict adherence to the restoration ideal. On the other hand, many of the Christians in the South held strictly to the restoration ideal as Campbell had expressed it in *The Christian Baptist* and resisted the fact of religious pluralism.

This theological rupture was rooted in the ambiguities of Campbell's own thought. We recall from chapter seven that the Campbells had learned from the Enlightenment that the surest way to Christian union was reducing religion to a set of essentials upon which all reasonable people might agree. But for the substance of that teaching, the Campbells turned to the primitive church depicted in Scripture—a Puritan theme which most Enlightenment thinkers had rejected as divisive. By combining Puritan and Enlightenment ideals in a common theological platform, therefore, the Campbells created an unstable and even volatile agenda.

Further, a variety of social factors including the Civil War exacerbated the rupture. By the end of the century the rupture became open division. In 1906, the United States Religious Census showed two churches rather than one: the Disciples of Christ, highly ecumenical and centralized in the Midwest, and the Churches of Christ, fundamentally restorationist and centralized in the upper South.

The fact that Churches of Christ emerged with extraordinary strength in the region once dominated by the freedom movement of Barton W. Stone is important. Churches of Christ, in fact, ultimately must trace their success in this region to the great numerical strength of the Stone movement long before anyone in that area had even heard of Alexander Campbell. Even more important, when the amorphous and structureless Stone tradition finally began absorbing the more regimented theology of Campbell after 1823, a subtle transition occurred: the reality of radical freedom slowly evolved into a rhetoric of radical freedom.

Eventually this rhetoric performed a double function. In the first place, it obscured from the eyes of these Christians the very real dogmas, forms, and structures that were developing in their midst. Put another way, their Common Sense perspectives rendered their emerging traditions essentially invisible, at least to themselves. When on occasion they recognized their traditions, moreover, they viewed them as essentially biblical, primitive, and apostolic and not in any sense the traditions of a particular people in a particular time and a particular place.

In the second place, the rhetoric of radical freedom finally became a dogma in its own right. In this way, their presumed lack of tradition became itself a tradition, their rejection of theology became a fundamental theological maxim, and their zeal to escape the constraints of history became the substance and core of the particular history of this particular people.

Since those early days, members of Churches of Christ often have assumed they are a people with no history and no tradition, a people whose only roots lie in the Bible itself. Yet Churches of Christ are heir to a long line of believers whose chief tradition has been their resistance to tradition. Born of the Christian Humanists of the fifteenth and sixteenth centuries, this tradition was refined by Reformed Protestants on the Continent, by Puritans in both Old and New England, and finally by Baptists and others on the American frontier. When this traditionless tradition finally took root among our forebearers, it already had a long and venerable history.

Looking Ahead

We now turn, in the chapters that follow, to three movements in Christian history whose perspectives on the task of restoration not only differed among themselves but also differed from our own.

We look first at Martin Luther who rejected out of hand any attempt to restore the primitive church since, in his view, restoration promoted a form of works righteousness that nullified both the grace of God and the blood of Christ.

Second, we examine the Anabaptist movement of the Reformation period. Anabaptists embraced the concept of restoration with extraordinary zeal, but had little concern for the forms and structures of primitive Christianity that were so important to our own forebearers. Rather, they preached a recovery of radical Christian discipleship.

And finally, we look at the Holiness and Pentecostal groups of our own time. They also have urged a restoration of apostolic Christianity; for them, however, apostolic Christianity grows from empowerment by the same Spirit that empowered the first Christians on the Day of Pentecost almost 2,000 years ago.

Then, in our final chapter, we ask what we might learn from all of this. What conclusions might we draw from learning the nature and trajectory of our own peculiar roots? And what can we learn from other restorationists whose focus has differed from our own?

Questions

1. Identify the four separate movements that emerged in the early years of the nineteenth century and that contributed to the Restoration Movement in which contemporary Churches of Christ have roots.

2. What was the principal motivation undergirding the work of James O'Kelly, Elias Smith, and Barton W. Stone?

3. When Barton W. Stone spoke of restoring primitive Christianity, what did he chiefly have in mind?

4. In what ways did Thomas Campbell, especially in his *Declaration and Address*, blend themes he had inherited both from the Puritans and from the Enlightenment? (See also chapter seven.)

5. In what ways did Alexander Campbell contrast with Barton W. Stone? Why did Campbell appeal so effectively to the "old Stoneite Christians"? How did Campbell help to transform the older Stone tradition in Kentucky and neighboring areas?

6. What finally caused the Campbell movement to break apart? What were the chief theological characteristics of the two segments? Geographically, where were the two segments located?

7. When did the United States Religious Census recognize the division, and how did the census designate the two wings of the movement?

8. What is the "double function" which the tradition and rhetoric of freedom has performed among Churches of Christ?

For Further Study

Garrett, Leroy. *The Stone-Campbell Movement: An Anecdotal History of Three Churches.* Joplin, MO: College Press, 1981.

Harrell, David Edwin, Jr. *Quest for a Christian America: The Disciples of Christ and American Society to 1866.* Nashville: Disciples of Christ Historical Society, 1966.

_____. "The Sectional Origins of the Churches of Christ." *Journal of Southern History* 30 (August 1964): 261–277.

_____. *The Social Sources of Division in the Disciples of Christ, 1865–1900.* Atlanta: Publishing Systems, Inc., 1973.

*Humble, Bill J. "The Restoration Ideal in the Churches of Christ." In *The American Quest for the Primitive Church.* Edited by Richard T. Hughes. Chicago and Urbana: University of Illinois Press, 1988.

_____. *The Story of the Restoration.* Austin: Firm Foundation, 1969.

Murch, James DeForest. *Christians Only.* Cincinnati: Standard Publishing, 1962.

Tucker, William E. and McAllister, Lester G. *Journey in Faith: A History of the Christian Church (Disciples of Christ).* St. Louis: The Bethany Press, 1975.

West, Earl Irvin. *The Search for the Ancient Order.* 4 vols. Indianapolis: Religious Book Service, 1950–1979; and Germantown, TN: Religious Book Service, 1987.

^{10/}Restoring the Gospel of Grace: Martin Luther

"Beware lest you make Christ into a Moses and the gospel into a book of law, as has been done before now . . . . Properly speaking, the gospel demands no works of us to become holy and redeemed. Indeed, it damns such works and requires of us only that we trust in Christ, because he has overcome sin, death, and hell for us."

MARTIN LUTHER

I n the preceding chapters we have traced the roots of Churches of Christ back to the Reformed tradition that emerged in the Reformation of the sixteenth century. We have seen in that tradition the focus on restoring the forms and structures of the apostolic church, and we have traced that approach to restoration through the Puritan movement and on into the stream of American religion.

Now in this chapter we return to the sixteenth century and look at a different perspective on the restoration of the church— that of Martin Luther (1483–1546). Chapter three briefly contrasted Luther with the Reformed theologians, but here we will explore his views at greater length, for Luther can help us see more clearly both the strengths and weaknesses of our traditional view of restoration.

In this chapter we ask: What drove Luther in his work as a reformer? How did Luther's view of the Bible differ from that of Zwingli and the Reformed theologians? How, according to Luther, does one identify the true church? And why did Luther oppose the restoration of biblical forms and structures?

Martin Luther: the great reformer of the sixteenth century who viewed justification by faith as the center of the Christian message. (sixteenth-century painting by Lucas Cranach; Imago Strahlbild)

Luther's Quest

Martin Luther was, above all, a man plagued with guilt. Luther trembled before a fierce God who sternly and righteously judged the universe, damning sinners to hell for the slightest infraction of his perfect law. The young Luther, therefore, lived in terror that this awesome and demanding God had rejected him. He feared that God had spurned his prayers, rejected his agonized repentance, and finally abandoned him to suffer the pains of hell.

With this perception of God, the fundamental question of Luther's life was clear: "How can I find the mercy and grace of God?" This was his ultimate quest. The young Luther concluded that he would simply make himself acceptable to God through good works and righteous living. In 1505, after a frightening brush with death, he decided to become a monk, reasoning that in the monastery it would be possible to live this righteous life, acceptable to God.

> I tried to live according to the Rule with all diligence, and I used to be contrite, to confess and number off my sins, and often repeated my confession, and sedulously performed my allotted penance. And yet my conscience could never give me certainty, but I always doubted and said, "You did not perform that correctly. You were not contrite enough. You left that out of your confession." The more I tried to remedy an uncertain, weak and afflicted conscience with the traditions of men, the more each day found it more uncertain, weaker, more troubled.

In 1512 the troubled Luther was assigned to teach a course in Romans at the new University of Wittenberg. He struggled over Romans 1:16–17 which speaks of the "gospel" or "good news." How can this be good news, Luther wondered, when God has set his face against me and nothing I can do seems to avert his wrath? But then in verse seventeen he read, "As it is written, the just shall live by faith."

He was thunderstruck: by faith, not by works; by faith, not by monastic austerity; by faith, not by the thoroughness of one's confession. It dawned on Luther that the gospel is "good news" precisely because one is saved by God's grace and not by works, and that one can accept this incredible gift only through faith.

Armed with this new conviction, Luther set out to challenge any and all who made God's love and acceptance dependent on human righteousness. He attacked indulgence salesmen who sold God's grace for a price. They made a mockery of God's grace, he felt, and in response to their claims he wrote the "Ninety-Five Theses" which would usher in the Protestant Reformation.

Luther also attacked those who sought to focus restoration on the forms and structures of the primitive church. Luther asked not, "What is the biblical pattern that I should imitate?" but rather, "How can I receive forgiveness of my sins?"

The Purpose of Scripture

This basic question shaped the way Luther read the Bible. He certainly believed that the Bible was the Word of God and that this

Word stood far above all human traditions. This conviction, in fact, formed the center of his theology. But he understood the nature of that Word differently than did the Reformed theologians. For Luther, the divine Word was spoken supremely in the person of Jesus Christ, not in a mere book. By "Word of God," therefore, he referred most often to the incarnate Christ, the Son of God. The Bible was the Word of God only in a secondary sense—only as it testified to Christ and made him present to us.

For Luther the Bible functioned much like a window in a house. The window functions to make the outside world visible and to let in light. It is possible, however, to so focus on the window that one fails to see beyond it. So with the Bible, Luther felt: it functions to reveal Christ to people, not to call attention to itself or to become an object of faith in itself.

Christ himself is supremely the Word of God, Luther argued, but this Word is mediated to us in three outward or visible forms: the Bible, the church, and the sacraments (baptism and the Lord's supper). When a person preaches the biblical message something extremely important takes place: the Holy Spirit activates Christ, the living Word, so that he works powerfully in the lives of those who hear the message. By itself the Bible is only a dead word. But when the Spirit works in conjunction with the preaching of the gospel, the Bible becomes a powerful, living Word, banishing the power of sin and evil.

When Luther proclaimed "Scripture alone" he always was proclaiming "Christ alone." As the Word of God, Scripture focuses on Christ and always turns around him as its center. Indeed, so strong was this emphasis that Luther could point to an inner canon of Scripture—a "canon within a canon" consisting of those writings that most clearly revealed Christ. He could speak, for example, of the epistle of James as an "epistle of straw" since it spoke very little of Christ and his redemptive work. For Luther, Scripture "must either refer to Christ or must not be held to be true Scriptures."

The True Church

Luther's Christ-centered approach to Scripture had profound implications for the attempt to distinguish the true church from the false.

The break with Rome had intensified Luther's questions about the church. What constituted a true church? And how was it to be recognized? Along with other reformers, Luther sought the "marks of the true church"; he could insist, like others, that one cannot simply claim to be the true church but must bear its marks. Thus he laid out seven identifying marks: the preaching of the gospel, baptism, the Lord's supper, the office of the keys (church discipline), the consecration of ministers, prayer and public praise, and faithfulness in suffering. With these as a standard, he could claim that "the original and ancient church shines forth once more. . . . Thus we have proved that we are the true, ancient church, one body and one communion of saints with the holy, universal, Christian Church."

Luther most certainly did not think, however, that by restoring these seven marks one thereby had restored the true church. The seven marks per se did not constitute the church. Luther insisted, in fact, that there is great danger in looking to external forms and patterns, for one is tempted to think that in restoring outward forms alone one has restored the essence. For Luther, the outward forms constitute only an empty shell.

Luther argued that the church is created only by the living Christ in the preaching of the gospel, not by any human work or achievement. He made this point repeatedly and insistently. Luther's passion was for the pure gospel of unmerited grace. Everything else was secondary. All the external marks and structures were expendable in restoring and preserving this gospel, this living Word, for "the Church is nothing without the Word and everything in it exists by virture of the Word alone," that is, the living Christ through whom God works powerfully in people's lives.

Luther believed that the preaching of this Word had formed and sustained the church, however corrupt, throughout the centuries. He simply could not dismiss the Roman Church with its corrupt traditions as no church at all, for Luther recognized his debt to the Roman Church. Through this tradition, after all, he had received the Scriptures and thus had been able to learn the gospel. Luther therefore did not look for the restoration of a church that had been entirely lost, but rather for the reformation of a church that had been seriously corrupted.

In view of the oppression and tyranny of the Roman Church—a church which he was led finally to identify explicitly with the "Antichrist"—Luther came to believe that the true church is a "hidden church." He meant by this term that the true church is not set apart and discernible because of its correct external marks—its name, works, offices, apostolic succession, and discipline—but rather because of its faith, a faith always stirred up by the preached Word. Indeed, a church may possess the outward marks of an apostolic church and yet be devoid of the gospel of God's redeeming grace.

The true church remains, in its essence, a hidden reality, living in tension with all institutional forms. For Luther the true, "hidden" church is part of the institutional, visible church, yet never identical with it. It is never identical, he insisted, because the true church, like the individual believer, has its essence in faith alone, not in works or in external forms. People are prone to put their trust in the visible institution and its forms rather than in the Christ who gives the church its life. They inevitably seek to identify the true church by means of perfect external forms and by its works, thus denying that the church lives only by grace through faith. But just as the individual is saved by grace, not by works, so too the church lives by grace, not by its perfect obedience and perfect institutional forms.

Reform of the Church

Luther's view of the hiddenness of the true church led him to reject and to warn against the mere imitation of biblical examples and patterns.

The first task of church renewal, Luther believed, was not restoration of biblical patterns, but rather restoration of the gospel message of divine grace, the recovery of the living Word through which faith was stirred up and through which believers received forgiveness and life. Fixation on biblical forms and patterns, he believed, too easily obscured the centrality of grace and faith.

Luther was not opposed to all biblical patterns and exemplary models; he could find in Scripture many great models of moral virture that could serve an educational function—figures like Moses, David, and Paul. But such exemplary models, he believed, applied primarily to the worldly kingdom, to one's existence as a citizen on this earth.

The Wittenberg Castle Church: the memorable site where Luther nailed his "Ninety-five Theses" on October 31, 1517. (photo by Everett Ferguson, Abilene, TX)

In the spiritual kingdom, on the other hand, where the central concern was prompting the spiritual life, Luther saw serious dangers in the imitation of biblical models. For one more readily sees the works or external features and imitates them rather than seeing the inner faith that motivated them. One gets absorbed in following the patterns and loses sight of the centrality of faith. For this reason, therefore, Luther viewed the effort to restore the patterns and traditions of primitive Christianity as fundamentally at odds with the gospel.

Luther's strong stand on this issue can be seen clearly in his reaction to what is called the Wittenberg Movement (1521–1522). Wittenberg was Luther's home and center of influence, but for a time he was away in hiding at the Wartburg Castle. While he was away, an associate of his named Andreas Bodenstein von Karlstadt (1480–1541) led a movement seeking further and more rapid reform of the German church.

Guiding Karlstadt's reform efforts was a view of the Bible different from Luther's. For him the Bible was primarily a divine law book providing patterns for the Christian life and for the church. Proper reform of the church, for him, thus meant stripping away immediately all of the ceremonies, traditions, and human laws associated with Roman Catholicism.

Karlstadt insisted, for example, that images be removed from the church building, that the bread (or host) not be elevated in the observance of the Lord's Supper, and that the terms "mass" and "sacrament" not be used. He objected to those things because they were not authorized by biblical law and did not characterize the primitive church. Karlstadt, in short, was a biblical restorationist, seeking to do away with all practices that did not conform to biblical prescript or example.

Learning of these efforts, Luther chastised Karlstadt severely. "Listen, murderer of souls and sinful spirit!" Luther thundered, "Are you not indeed a murderer of souls who sets himself above us in God's place and takes away our Christian liberty and subordinates consciences to himself?" He continued with the charge that such an approach creates a new legalism, that it "destroys faith, profanes the blood of Christ, blasphemes the gospel, and sets all that Christ has won for us at nought. . . ." Such restorationism, Luther believed, placed human effort above God's grace and was therefore the worst sort of idolatry.

In Luther's view, the external act or pattern set forth in Scripture is not to be imitated. Rather, the inner significance (faith) is to be appropriated. "We do not want to follow any example," he wrote; rather, "we want the Word for the sake of which all works, examples, and miracles occur." For him the essence of Christianity had very little to do with biblical forms susceptible to progressive change through time.

We can even go so far as to say that, for Luther, there was no "fall" of the church, if by "fall" we mean a sudden break in history when the true church was lost. He did believe that the church had declined from its original glory and that the early age of martyrs was the "springtime" of the church. But Luther understood the church's fall in the sense of apostasy, that is, not as the loss of some original pattern but rather as a falling into error and an establishing of a community opposed to the true church. The church had fallen into error and needed to be purged, but it had not ceased to exist.

Here was the key point for Luther. The continuity of the church did not rest in institutional guarantees or in externally visible marks. It rested, rather, in the sustaining power of God through his Word, a power that lay beyond the church itself and that always stood in judgment on the church. Luther wrote:

> God alone is able to keep the church alive, as he has done so wonderfully since the beginning of the world, in the midst of great weakness, division caused by sects and heresies, and persecution by tyrants. He alone rules the church, although he commits and uses the ministry of people to administer His word and sacrament.

With such a view, Luther could face the often tragic realities of the church's existence in history—the blemishes, divisions, and ruptures. He could see all the confusion and, in the midst of it, share the agony and the struggles of Christ's body. Such struggles would continue, he believed, because of the perpetual clash between the "twofold church," between those living under the Word and those without it. For Luther the early age of the church was not an ideal age to which those in the present must return. Rather, the early period of the church simply presented, through glimpses into the pioneers' triumphs and struggles of faith, the "enduring face" of the church for every period.

Conclusion

Luther's view of the church and its renewal differed radically from that of a restorationist. Luther simply did not ask the question that was fundamental to all Christian restorationists, namely, "What was the ancient tradition or pattern?" Rather, he raised what was to him the most fundamental question of all, "How can I find a gracious and merciful God?"

There is a sense, to be sure, in which Luther was a restorationist. For as he himself once put it, "the crawling maggots of man-made laws and regulations" had "eaten into the entire world" and had "swallowed up . . . all Holy Scripture." Thus, Luther sought to go behind the "man-made laws and regulations" of history to preach once again the primitive gospel of faith and grace.

From this perspective, Luther perhaps could be called a "gospel restorationist." But the essence of that gospel, in Luther's view, was God's activity, not that of human beings, and this was the point that made all the difference. Once the gospel had been proclaimed, therefore, Luther sought not so much to recover apostolic forms or traditions as simply to receive by faith the grace whereby God forgave his sins and enabled him to stand.

Questions

1. What was the fundamental question that lay at the foundation of Luther's reform movement? What made this such a burning question for him? What answer did he find?

2. When Luther urged "Scripture alone," what did he mean? How did Luther's focus differ from Zwingli and the Reformed theologians? How does it differ from the traditional view among Churches of Christ?

3. How did Luther answer the question, "Where is the true church?" Did he think the true church had any identifying marks? If so, how important were they? How have Churches of Christ sought to identify the true church?

4. Why was Luther not willing to dismiss the Roman Catholic Church as a completely false church?

5. What point was Luther making when he contrasted the visible, institutional church with the faithful but "hidden" church?

6. Why did Luther oppose focusing restoration on biblical forms and structures? What should one focus on instead? What might Luther's concern at this point have to say to members of Churches of Christ?

7. How did Luther deal with the blemishes and divisions that had wracked the church throughout the ages? How should we view them today?

For Further Study

Althaus, Paul. *The Theology of Martin Luther*. Philadelphia: Fortress Press, 1966.

*Dillenberger, John, ed. *Martin Luther: Selections from His Writings*. Garden City, NY: Doubleday, 1961.

*Kittelson, James M. *Luther the Reformer: The Story of the Man and His Career*. Minneapolis: Augsburg, 1986.

Lotz, David. "*Sola Scriptura:* Luther on Biblical Authority." *Interpretation* 35 (July 1981): 258-73.

Pelikan, Jaroslav. *Luther the Expositor: Introduction to the Reformer's Exegetical Writings*. St. Louis: Concordia, 1959.

_____, and Lehmann, Helmut, eds. *Luther's Works*. American Edition. Philadelphia and St. Louis: Fortress and Concordia, 1955-1986.

Sider, Ronald J. *Andreas Bodenstein von Karlstadt: Documents in a Liberal-Radical Debate*. Philadelphia: Fortress, 1978.

*Steinmetz, David C. "Luther against Luther" and "Luther and the Two Kingdoms." In *Luther in Context*. Bloomington: Indiania University Press, 1986.

Watson, Philip J. *Let God Be God: An Interpretation of the Theology of Martin Luther*. 1947; reprint ed., Philadelphia: Fortress Press, 1966.

¹¹/Restoring an Apostolic Lifestyle: Anabaptists

"No one can be a profitable member in this ... pure body of Christ who is not believing, regenerate, converted, changed, and renewed; who is not kind, generous, merciful, pitying, chaste, sober, humble, patient, long-suffering, just, constant, heavenly and spiritually minded with Christ."

MENNO SIMONS (1539)

On January 21, 1525, in the city of Zurich, Switzerland, Conrad Grebel baptized George Blaurock, and thus performed the first adult baptism of the Reformation era.

That baptism launched one of the most important restoration movements in the entire history of Christianity. It was, however, a movement distinctly unlike our own in several fundamental respects. The thousands who became involved in this movement called themselves simply "brethren." Their opponents, however, labelled them "Anabaptists," and it was this name that stayed with them for many years.

That label—Anabaptist—is the key to understanding the genius of this movement to restore the apostolic faith.

The Union of Church and State

To understand that label we must turn the clock back some 1,200 years to the days of Constantine, Roman Emperor in the early fourth century A.D. After three centuries of sporadic and sometimes vicious persecutions launched against Christians,

Constantine embraced the Christian faith, placed it on an equal footing legally with all other religions in the empire, and extended favoritism to Christianity in a variety of ways. With Constantine the days of the Christian martyrs had ended.

Theodosius, emperor from 379 to 385, took Constantine's favor toward Christianity even further, making Christianity the only legitimate religion of the empire. He decreed in 380 that all who refused this faith would "suffer... the punishment which our authority . . . shall decide to inflict."

These new policies wrought a dramatic change for the Christian faith. Suddenly, Christians ceased to be a people under the cross, hunted, persecuted, and killed. Rather, Christianity became a faith of power and prestige. If one aspired to high political office or success in business or any other pursuit, he knew he must first demonstrate loyalty as a Christian. Over the centuries, the church grew wealthy and the popes grew politically powerful—developments that are too well known to need repeating here.

In the days prior to Constantine, the Christian faith required self-conscious commitment. Indeed, to be a Christian was a life and death proposition. Many were arrested, mutilated, and often killed. No one became a Christian for social reasons. But in the years and centuries following the Constantinian settlement, the Christian profession often cost little or nothing at all. Everyone in the Holy Roman Empire was at least nominally Christian, since everyone had been baptized in infancy. And many took the Christian profession with little seriousness.

By 1500, on the eve of the Protestant Reformation, a church which required little serious commitment on the part of its members had perpetuated itself for well over 1,000 years. The result was a church wracked with immorality and ignorance. Drunkenness and sexual promiscuity was not uncommon, even among priests. The buying and selling of church offices had become lucrative business, as had the buying of one's salvation through the purchase of indulgences. Simply put, the world had invaded the church to such an enormous extent that there was little difference left between the two.

The arrangement that perpetuated this state of affairs is commonly known as the state-church. Everyone in a given nation belonged to the church by virtue of infant baptism. The state exalted the church with privilege and power, and the church in turn rendered homage to the state. By 1500, this arrangement had been in place for so long that few in Europe even thought to question it.

Even the great reformers—Luther, Calvin, and Zwingli—accepted the state-church principle. They deplored the immoralities that afflicted the church, but refused to call for a church that would separate itself from the world's priorities, privileges, and power. Their assumption—virtually universal in Europe at the time—was that no nation could be viable without one official church that encompassed the nation's entire population.

The Anabaptist Commitment

Precisely at this point the Anabaptists took their stand. For them, it was far more important to have a living, pure church than to have a viable state. They deplored the immoralities that ran rampant in the church of their time and longed for commitment and dedication, for a church that would embody purity of life and singleness of purpose. They compared the church of their day with the church described in the New Testament, and they knew precisely where their own commitment lay.

The Anabaptists' commitment to the purity of the apostolic faith was sparked in Zurich by the preaching of the great Reformed theologian, Huldreich Zwingli (see chapter three). Zwingli had proclaimed the importance of returning to the sources of the Christian faith—the teachings of Jesus and the apostles, embodied in Scripture itself.

To some who heard Zwingli preach, a return to Scripture should also entail a return to the lifestyle of radical discipleship which Scripture taught. But it was apparent to these believers that a lifestyle of radical discipleship would mean an end to the centuries-old state-church alliance. Since this alliance was maintained by infant baptism, they called on Zwingli, therefore, to reject infant baptism and to preach the baptism of believing, committed adults.

In keeping with the state-church arrangement, Zwingli referred this question to the town council which judged against such a radical proposal. In the council's eyes, the proclamation of adult baptism would disrupt both church and state and would therefore be seditious, if not revolutionary, in its implications. Zwingli, therefore, refused to heed the call of the radicals for a restoration of believer's baptism. Conrad Grebel, the leader of the radicals, complained,

> Your shepherds have often asserted that the Scriptures must be allowed to speak for themselves to which we may not add nor subtract anything. Although this was the intention it was never carried out.... [I] am sure that ... [Zwingli] has exactly this same understanding of baptism.... [I] do not know . . . for what reason he does not declare himself.

This small band of believers determined—in spite of the negative response of Zwingli and the council—to embrace a lifestyle consistent with Scripture and to signify this commitment by submission to believer's baptism. Thus it was that on January 21, 1525, Grebel poured water over the head of George Blaurock and the Anabaptist movement was born.

While many of these believers ultimately practiced immersion, the term "Anabaptist" itself signified only re-baptism—the re-baptism of adults who had been baptized already as infants. But most important, their opponents hurled this label at the radicals with relentless rage.

Why did the simple act of re-baptism of believers so infuriate the people and their magistrates? It is true that these radicals sought to take Scripture as their only guide to faith and practice. That alone, however, caused them no trouble. What generated wrath was their conviction that biblical faith entailed a life of radical discipleship—purity of heart, holy living, and commitment to Christ regardless of the consequences.

Such a conviction obviously meant a separation from the state-church which embraced reprobates, open sinners, and even unbelievers with ease. Adult baptism, therefore, was a symbol of their separation from the established order. And separation implicitly was judgment on the commonly accepted state-church arrangement.

Persecution

In the years that followed, the established order unleashed a hail of fury upon the Anabaptists that would mark their story as one of the great stories of faith and martyrdom in the history of the Christian faith. Indeed, their insistence on baptizing adults allowed the authorities to revive an ancient Roman law which prescribed death for re-baptizers (in this case, the Donatists).

An early woodcut showing the torture and death of Anabaptists: "They would die ten deaths rather than forsake the divine truth."

Thus, the emperor at the Diet of Speyer in 1529 invoked this ancient Justinian Code, thereby making Anabaptists fair game for imprisonment, torture, and death all over Europe.

Interestingly, Anabaptists suffered not only at the hands of the magistrates and the Catholic Church—the traditional established order; major Protestant reformers also called for their extermination. In fact, almost everyone turned against the Brethren in a wholesale war of extinction, sparing no form of torture and death. One of the early leaders wrote:

> Some they have executed by hanging, some they have tortured with inhuman tyranny, and afterwards choked with cords at the stake. Some they roasted and burned alive. Some they have killed with the sword and given them to the fowls of the air to devour. Some they have cast to the fishes.... Others wander about here and there, in want, homelessness, and affliction, in mountains and deserts, in holes and caves of the earth. They must flee with their wives and little children from one country to another, from one city to another. They are hated, abused, slandered and lied about by all men.

The persecution thus loosed made their witness all the more meaningful. From the beginning they had called for lives of dedication and commitment in spite of the consequences. They now suffered the deadly consequences, and in most cases their commitment to Christ and to holy and righteous living persisted to the end. An Anabaptist chronicler, after reporting the deaths of 2173 of his brothers and sisters, commented on their faith: "The fire of God burned within them. They would die ten deaths rather than forsake the divine truth. They had drunk of the water which is flowing from God's sanctuary, yea of the water of life. Their tent they had pitched not here upon earth, but in eternity."

The Meaning of Restoration

By the mid-1530s, Anabaptists were scattered and discouraged. The persecution had borne fruit. In 1536, however, a Dutch Roman Catholic priest named Menno Simons, deeply moved by the simple evangelical faith of these people and their sufferings, renounced his Catholicism, embraced the faith of the Anabaptists, and soon emerged as the shepherd of this scattered flock.

In the many epistles he addressed to the scattered Brethren, Menno—more than anyone else—explained the meaning of the simple faith which the Brethren embraced. He made clear what the Brethren meant when they spoke of restoration or recovery of primitive Christianity.

The Brethren did indeed employ the concept of restoration with great regularity. The established church, Menno wrote, was a "worldly church" and "has left her lawful husband, Christ, and follows after strange lovers." He sought, therefore, "to reclaim this adulterous bride . . . and return her to her first husband." In a particularly illuminating statement, Menno wrote that

> since it is as clear as the noonday sun that for many centuries no difference has been visible between the church and the world, . . . we are constrained . . . to gather together . . . a pious and penitent congregation or church out of all impure and deceiving sects of the world . . . .

Like Luther, Menno and his colleagues did not emphasize the forms, structures, and rites of the apostolic church. But neither did they concern themselves principally with the theology of faith and grace that meant so much to Luther. Rather, the restoration of the Anabaptists was first and foremost an ethical, behavioral restoration.

While insisting on adult baptism, for example, the Anabaptists rigorously denied that outward baptism makes one a Christian. Indeed, they rejected fellowship with the baptized who had not committed themselves to holy and righteous living. Menno wrote that all who were "quarrelsome, tumultuous, slanderous, defaming, bitter, wrathful, and cruel of heart" were not "in His kingdom, even though they do carry the external appearance of being Christians, and are greeted as brethren." What made one a Christian was a changed life. In 1539, Menno declared that

> no one can be a profitable member in this . . . pure body of Christ who is not believing, regenerate, converted, changed, and renewed; who is not kind, generous, merciful, pitying, chaste, sober, humble, patient, long-suffering, just, constant, heavenly and spiritually minded with Christ.

Another leader, Balthasar Hubmaier, endorsed this credo. For him, baptism was a pledge to a new life of righteousness and purity. The baptismal candidate "has purposed and pledged himself in heart henceforth to lead another and a better life," Hubmaier wrote. "He shall testify this publicly when he receives the water of baptism."

Righteousness and purity entailed for the Brethren a radical separation from the values and ways of the world. Thus, no Anabaptist could serve as a ruler or magistrate in an earthly kingdom—a calling the Brethren viewed as diametrically opposed to service in the kingdom of Christ. The Brethren also proclaimed a rigorous pacifism and refused to fight under any circumstances. This meant, of course, that they met persecution, torture, and even death with absolute non-resistance. To the Brethren, non-resistance was simply the Master's chosen path.

More than this, during the period of intense persecution the Brethren taught that one's life should be willingly given for another. They even celebrated this theme in the Lord's Supper. Balthasar Hubmaier made this plain: "Through the breaking of bread and pouring of wine, there is a spiritual indication that each of us should be willing to offer his flesh and blood for his fellows." As Christ had poured himself out for the world, so the Brethren should pour themselves out for one another, "even to the offering of our bodies, lives, property, [and] blood for their sakes."

Menno Simons: Anabaptist leader who sought to gather morally pure congregations out of a corrupt established church. (Mennonite Historical Library, Goshen College, Goshen, Indiana)

Their preoccupation with a pure and holy church also explains the Anabaptists' concern for the rigorous exercise of church discipline. A candidate for baptism had to promise to submit to exclusion should he or she become entangled once again with the world. While one purpose of the ban was to reclaim the errant believer, it also was intended to preserve the purity of the church. Menno wrote that sinful members should be excluded "lest the others be corrupted and the ugly scurvy be transmitted to other sheep." And Dietrich Philips asserted that "if open sinners, transgressors, and the disorderly are not excluded, the whole congregation must be defiled (1 Cor. 5:13; 1 Thess. 5:14), and if false brethren are retained, we become partakers of their sins." In such a case, the separatist congregations of the Anabaptists would become no better than the inclusive church of the larger society.

Thus, the ban was fundamental to restoring the purity of pre-Constantinian Christianity. Menno himself placed the ban squarely in the context of the restoration ideal: "The ban was so diligently practiced, first by Christ Jesus and his apostles, and afterward by us, who are intent upon recovering again Christian doctrine and practice . . . ." At the heart of Anabaptism lay its concern to restore the holy and righteous living that had characterized Christianity in apostolic days.

Differences Between Anabaptists and Churches of Christ

Members of Churches of Christ may be surprised to learn what restoration did *not* mean to these Anabaptists. The Brethren paid little attention to the various forms and structures that have been important to Churches of Christ in America in the nineteenth and twentieth centuries. There is, for example, little evidence that Brethren concerned themselves with matters of church organization. Their chief concern instead was for the rule of Christ in the lives of the believers. And while the Brethren said little about the frequency of the Lord's Supper, they spoke much of its meaning and significance. Further, while they often practiced immersion, their first concern was for the baptism of adults who would commit themselves without reservation to the way of the cross.

How can we account for the difference in emphasis between ourselves and the Brethren some 450 years ago? Surely that difference cannot be ascribed to a lack of interest on the part of either group in the recovery of primitive Christianity. To recapture authentic, primitive Christianity was a driving theme of both movements.

Where, then, does the difference lie? Fundamentally, the difference exists in differing views of the Bible informed by radically differing social, cultural, and intellectual circumstances. The Anabaptists, reacting against a church that had become captive to the world, looked to the Bible as a guide to righteous and holy living. They were not concerned with the unity of Christians as was Alexander Campbell. They were concerned instead for separation from the world and from so-called Christians whose lives were dominated by the world. Further, the

Anabaptists had not experienced the Enlightenment of the late seventeenth and eighteenth centuries, and therefore had no inclination to view the Bible as a kind of scientific blueprint or constitution. The Bible answered the questions they asked, and the questions they asked had to do with faith, holiness, and separation from the world.

On the other hand, Alexander Campbell, the moving force of our own movement in the nineteenth century, was far less concerned with separation from the world than he was with the unity of all Christians. His background was not the moral laxity of medieval Catholicism, but rather the sectarian divisiveness of Protestantism. It was to this that Campbell chiefly responded. Further, Campbell and all the early leaders of our movement were immersed in the assumptions of the eighteenth-century Enlightenment. Thus, Campbell was inclined to see the Bible far more as a blueprint for church organization and worship than as a guide to holy living, though he obviously was not uninterested in the latter.

Conclusion

One final note concerning the Anabaptists: as the Brethren increasingly recognized Menno Simons as their shepherd and leader, the term "Mennonite" increasingly became the common designation for these followers of Christ. Then, by the 1690s, a time when many Mennonite congregations had grown lax in their enforcement of the ban, Jakob Ammann, a Swiss Mennonite, led a schism which focused on that issue and on the question of whether merely true-hearted people would be saved. Those who followed Ammann became known as Amish Mennonites, and many today are called simply Amish. A third major group, the Hutterites, descend from the followers of Jakob Hutter who shepherded the Brethren in Moravia during the earliest years of the Anabaptist witness. This wing is less well known in America than are Amish and Mennonites, though numerous Hutterite colonies continue in Montana and the Dakotas, as well as in Alberta and Manitoba, Canada.

The original Anabaptist witness continues today among Amish, Mennonites, and Hutterites. These people continue to separate from the world for the sake of living out a simple

Christian faith patterned after the teachings of Christ and the apostles. They persist in making rigorous demands on their members, practicing the ban, refusing political and military involvement, and giving themselves for one another in countless forms of mutual aid. They exemplify yet another meaning of the concept, "restoration of primitive Christianity."

Questions

1. What was the central focus of the Anabaptist restoration?

2. How did the Anabaptist restoration differ from the Restoration Movement of which Churches of Christ are a part?

3. How can one account for those differences? What impact might one's cultural and intellectual environment have on his or her view of the Bible?

4. Why were Anabaptists so concerned for righteous and holy living?

5. Why were Anabaptists viewed as seditious and revolutionary, and why were they the objects of such fierce persecution?

6. What can Churches of Christ learn from the witness of the Brethren of the sixteenth century?

For Further Study

*Durnbaugh, Donald. *The Believers' Church: The History and Character of Radical Protestantism.* New York: Macmillan, 1968.

_____, ed. *Every Need Supplied: Mutual Aid and Christian Community in the Free Churches, 1525–1675.* Philadelphia: Temple University Press, 1974.

Estep, William R. *The Anabaptist Story.* Nashville: Broadman Press, 1963.

Hughes, Richard T. "Christian Primitivism as Perfectionism: From Anabaptists to Pentecostals." In *Reaching Beyond: Chapters in the History of Perfectionism.*, pp. 212–55. Edited by Stanley Burgess. Peabody, MA: Hendrickson Publishers, 1986.

*Hughes, Richard T. "A Comparison of the Restitution Motifs of the Campbells (1809–1830) and the Anabaptists (1524–1560)." *Mennonite Quarterly Review* 45 (October 1971):312–330.

Littell, Franklin H. *The Origins of Sectarian Protestantism.* New York: Macmillan, 1964.

MacMaster, Richard K. *Land, Piety, and Peoplehood: The Establishment of Mennonite Communities in America, 1683–1790.* Scottdale, PA: Herald Press, 1985.

The Mennonite Encyclopedia, 4 vols. Scottdale, PA: Mennonite Publishing House, 1955.

Wenger, John C. *Separated Unto God: A Plea for Christian Simplicity of Life and for a Scriptural Nonconformity to the World.* Scottdale, PA: Mennonite Publishing House, 1952.

Williams, George Hunston. *The Radical Reformation.* Philadelphia: Westminster Press, 1962.

12/Restoring Life in the Spirit: Holiness and Pentecostal Advocates

"The Pentecostal Movement . . . leaps the intervening years crying, 'Back to Pentecost'. . . . [It does] not recognize a doctrine or custom as authoritative unless it can be traced to that primal source of church instruction, the Lord and his apostles."

B. F. LAWRENCE (1916)

Many movements in Christian history have self-consciously committed themselves to the restoration of primitive Christianity. Strikingly, however, these various movements have differed, sometimes significantly, in their understandings of just what should be restored.

So far in our review, we have seen that Puritans, Baptists, and some of our own forebearers focused the restoration lens especially on the forms and structures of the primitive church. Typically, these leaders were themselves uncertain just which forms and which structures required restoration.

Others, like the Anabaptists and the early Stone Christians, had a different focus. They concerned themselves not so much with forms and structures but rather with the character of the earliest Christian saints. Still others, like the early Mormons, sought to restore to a latter-day church the same direct communication with God that had characterized God's people in ancient days.

In more recent years, holy living and spiritual empowerment have been central themes of two self-consciously restorationist movements in America. The quest to recover holy living was the burden of the Holiness movement which began in the late nineteenth century, while restoration of spiritual empowerment motivated the people who came to be known as Pentecostals early in this century.

Vital commonalities linked the Holiness and Pentecostal groups, commonalities which had their beginnings among the Methodists of England in the early eighteenth century.

Methodist Revival

The Church of England, by the early eighteenth century, had become the religious incarnation of the Age of Reason. Proper, cultured, and orderly, it tamed emotion and exalted reason in both preaching and liturgy. Accordingly, the Church of England lost much of its popular support among the masses and became the church of the educated, the wealthy, and the elite.

These developments distressed no one more than John Wesley (1703– 1791), a loyal child of the Church of England. Knowing that most English people had abandoned church attendance, Wesley determined to take the church to the people. He preached to whomever would listen—workers in fields and factories, miners at their mines, gatherings in village streets.

Wesley preached a message that spoke to the heart, not just to the head. Wesley's two-fold message proclaimed first that the blood of Christ and the grace of God freely justified Christians, and second, that the Spirit empowered Christians to live holy and sanctified lives.

As Wesley attracted a following, he organized people into "societies"—small groups given to a methodically rigorous schedule of Bible study and prayer. By this means, Wesley taught, one could remain open to spiritual empowerment and holy living. This methodical cultivation of holiness brought Wesley and his followers the nick-name, "Methodists."

Wesley urged his followers to remain in the established Church of England, but he also encouraged them to observe a lifestyle that could only be viewed as separatist. The Methodists, Wesley taught, should avoid even the most subtle appearances of evil, shunning fashionable clothing, cursing, drunkenness, sensuous literature, and worldly music, not to mention murder, adultery, lying, and thieving.

These separatist tendencies eventually produced outright departure from the Church of England. By 1759, Wesley's sizeable, grass-roots movement was commonly called the Methodist Church, and in 1784, Wesley ordained Thomas Coke the first bishop of that body.

In America, Methodists took the frontier by storm. They succeeded astoundingly well because they, like Wesley in England, refused to wait for the people. Methodists dispatched hundreds of circuit riders who spared no effort in preaching even to the most isolated frontier people and who often rode to new settlement areas even before the pioneers themselves.

And Methodists brought with them to America the high ethical standards Wesley had taught them in England. Their neighbors knew them well by their commitment to holy living and their rejection of worldly values.

Methodist Decline

In the years following the Civil War, however, the Methodist commitment to holiness and sanctity began to wane, especially in the northern states. Those states had prospered from the war as post-war affluence brought significant new material blessings to many in that region. Some, like John D. Rockefeller, Andrew Carnegie, and John Pierpont Morgan, took advantage of the opportunities of their age to build immense personal fortunes. Others experienced, at the very least, a higher standard of living than they had known during antebellum years. Yet, beneath the patina of wealth lay the corruption that money attracts. For these reasons, historians speak of the post-Civil War years as the Gilded Age.

The promise of the Gilded Age seduced many Protestant denominations into social and economic acculturation. Many among Methodists, Baptists, Presbyterians—and even within our own movement—became far more enchanted with the modern age than with the primitive church. Success, prosperity, and the entrepreneurial spirit all too often left little room for simple and holy living.

The signs of this transition were unmistakeable. The churches rushed to construct ornate and costly sanctuaries where choirs and organs replaced unadorned congregational singing and where dramatic presentations and church festivals competed with secular organizations for the time and money of the cultured middle class. The noted evangelical A. J. Gordon observed the "new organs and frescoings and furnishings and . . . strawberry festivals" of the Protestant churches and drew a striking contrast between primitive and modern Christianity: "Is not this an infinite descent from the primitive records of power and suc-cess—the Lord 'confirming the word with signs following,' and . . .'in demonstration of the Spirit and of power?'"

One of the wits of our own movement, Fletcher Srygley, wryly described the same problem in our own churches in 1891. Srygley recalled that

> a friend of mine asked a highly respectable and strictly moral but irrelig-ious man why he did not go to church, and the man said he stayed away from such places out of respect for his deceased old mother who was a deeply pious woman and who always taught him never to attend places of fashionable amusement on Sunday.

This spiritual decline particularly touched Methodism, since for many years its hallmark had been zeal for holy living. As early as the 1830s, one bishop noted that the theme of holiness within Methodism was receiving "less and less attention . . . [and was in] danger of being regarded as a novelty." By 1866, primitive holi-ness stood increasingly at odds with an acculturated mainstream Methodism. In fact, some Methodists boldly rejoiced that "our church members have as a body risen in the social scale, and thus become socially removed from the great body out of which most of them were originally gathered."

The Holiness Revival

Following the Civil War, concerned Methodists organized themselves into a "Holiness Association" which launched the first "National Camp Meeting for the Promotion of Holiness" in 1867. They hoped this meeting would help rekindle the passion for holy living among Methodists. The meeting was a great success and spawned at least fifty-two national camp meetings from 1867 to 1883. For a while it appeared that Methodists would renew their commitment to sanctification.

By the 1880s, however, the doctrine of holiness had become a bone of contention in Methodist ranks. In the first place, the

"Holiness Association," dominated by Methodists but clearly interdenominational, had taken on a life of its own independent of Methodist ecclesiastical jurisdiction. Many Methodist leaders therefore attacked the holiness movement and sought to bring it under denominational control.

This action only alienated holiness advocates even further, and some now called for separation from the Methodist Church and the creation of separate holiness churches. John P. Brooks, who had been a Methodist for many years, felt betrayed by what he perceived as Methodism's growing accomodation to the world. He left the Methodist Church in 1885 and helped lead the "come-outism" movement which pulled many of the more radical holiness advocates completely out of Methodist ranks. Brooks no doubt spoke for many of his colleagues when he roundly condemned the "easy, indulgent, accomodating, mammonized" sort of Methodism that erects "gorgeous and costly temples to gratify its pride."

John Wesley had always taught and Methodists had always believed that sanctification was a work of the Holy Spirit, not a product of human will and effort. Wesley never stressed, however, that sanctification was particularly sudden or dramatic. For Wesley a Christian might simply grow into greater and greater holiness, led by the Spirit of God.

Those involved in the "come-outism" movement, however, went beyond Wesley and claimed that sanctification was a dramatic and sudden experience, wrought by the baptism of the Holy Ghost. The radical holiness leaders taught, therefore, that justification was the first work of grace whereby the Spirit of God cleansed and forgave the believer, and that sanctification was a second work of grace whereby the Spirit redirected the believer's life toward holiness and eventual perfection. This peculiar language—"first work of grace" and "second work of grace"—became central to the Holiness movement.

Methodist leaders increasingly viewed the Holiness movement as disruptive and proceeded to discipline holiness dissenters. They even required every Methodist bishop to take a stand for or against the holiness heresy.

MC GAVOCK BLOCK
NASHVILLE,TENN.

Robert Lee Harris: leader of the New Testament Church of Christ which merged with other Holiness churches in 1914 to form the Church of the Nazarene. (Nazarene Archives, Kansas City)

New Holiness Churches

Clearly the stage was set for the proliferation of "Holiness" denominations. Most of the new Holiness churches made their appeal in explicitly restorationist terms. They regularly contrasted the worldly commitments of Methodism with the sanctified lifestyle of the primitive Christians. They appealed beyond early Methodism to the first Christian age and viewed that age as the standard for Christian life and character.

Somewhat typical was a relatively obscure Holiness denomination organized in the very heartland of Churches of

Christ. Calling itself the New Testament Church of Christ, this Holiness denomination centered its activity in Milan, Tennessee in the east and Buffalo Gap, Texas (near Abilene) in the west.

The New Testament Church of Christ began when the West Tennessee Conference of the Methodist Episcopal Church, South, attacked "unauthorized, self-styled evangelists." Robert Lee Harris, a transplanted west Texan, in turn attacked Methodism as "fashionable and worldly" and set about establishing what he called a true "New Testament church." With the Bible as its only creed, elders governing, deacons serving tables, and both men and women preaching the word, Harris' church also instituted pouring for baptism and sanctification as a second work of grace. It rejected all flirtations with the world including jewelry, tobacco, secret societies, and idle amusements. In 1914, the New Testament Church of Christ merged with several other Holiness groups to form the Church of the Nazarene, today one of the major Holiness denominations.

Religious pluralism in America deeply troubled many Holiness advocates, just as it had Mormons and adherents to the Campbell-Stone movement some fifty years before. And like Mormons and Christians, many Holiness denominations viewed themselves as agents of the Christian unity which in turn would launch the millennial age.

Daniel S. Warner and his Church of God (Anderson, Indiana, 1880) is a notable case in point. Warner rejected the denominational pattern out of hand and summoned the true sheep of God out of their denominational structures and into "the only holy church of the Bible." To this point, Warner sounded remarkably like Alexander Campbell. But there was one fundamental difference.

Campbell sought to eradicate pluralism and unite God's people by recovering the doctrines, forms, and structures of the primitive church. The Holiness people, however, sought Christian unity by restoring the sanctified lifestyle of the primitive Christians, inaugurated by the baptism of the Holy Ghost.

Holiness advocates, in fact, typically rejected restoration efforts like Campbell's and viewed them as incapable of generating any Christian union at all. Edgar M. Levy proclaimed:

> At last we have discovered the basis for Christian unity. The sanctification of believers of every name, create unity in the great Christian brotherhood, such as no creed has ever been able to accomplish. [Here is] a unity not in

ordinances; a unity not in church government; a unity not in forms of worship; a unity not in mere letter or creed—but in . . . the baptism of the holy Spirit.

In pointing to Holy Ghost baptism as the basis for Christian union, Levy and his colleagues expressed their deep conviction that Christian union could not be achieved by human contrivance or manipulation, no matter how well intentioned, but only by the power of God. The radical holiness advocates contended that God alone could launch authentic restoration. Restoration designed by human beings and promoted by human beings, even if biblically based, was bound to fail.

Further, Levy and his colleagues maintained that restoration could not be cognitive or mechanical, but must be ethical and even experiential. Holiness churches, in fact, typically downplayed doctrine in the face of the sanctified Christian life. Hannah Whitall Smith, author of the devotional classic, *The Christian's Secret of a Happy Life* (1870), argued that "the trouble with most of the religion of the day is its extreme complexity," adding that true religion avoids "theological difficulties [and] doctrinal dilemmas . . . . No theological *training nor any especial theological views* are needed."

Daniel Warner agreed. He longed for the union of all Christians, "not bound together by rigid articles of faith, but perfectly united in love, under the primitive glory of the Sanctifier . . . ." For Warner and his co-religionists, the clear link between sanctification and Christian union was love, love that would dispel from the heart the selfish interests which built and sustained the denominational creeds and parties in the first place.

Through the power of the Spirit the millennial age of unity, peace, and harmony would be realized at last. But in the minds of Holiness advocates, that millennial age would be but a replication of the first age of the Christian faith when the Holy Spirit wrought holiness in the lives of disciples.

The Pentecostal Movement

Near the turn of the twentieth century, the Pentecostal movement grew directly out of Holiness longings for recovery of apostolic Christianity. But if the Holiness followers emphasized an ethical restoration, concerned chiefly with a sanctified way of

The Azusa Street Mission in Los Angeles: historic site where in 1906 William Seymour, a disciple of Charles Parham, began the revival that launched the modern Pentecostal movement. (Assemblies of God Archives, Springfield, Missouri)

life, Pentecostals sought to restore the apostolic gifts of the Spirit, particularly glossolalia (speaking in tongues) and healing.

Pentecostals especially sought the gifts of the Spirit in order to know whether the sanctified life, so coveted by Holiness advocates, was really the fruit of the Holy Spirit or the fruit of one's own striving. If holiness was the fruit of the Spirit, they reasoned, then one empowered by the Spirit should manifest the Spirit's presence in other ways as well.

Second, Pentecostals believed that sanctification and speaking in tongues were inseparable in the lives of the earliest Christians. From their perspective, the Holiness restoration was incomplete. To restore holiness apart from other gifts of the Spirit was to recover only part of the primitive Christian faith. Pentecostals, then, intended nothing less than a complete restoration of the Spirit's activity in the lives of God's people.

Further, since the Spirit empowered the Christians first in Jerusalem on the day of Pentecost, the "pentecostal" experience became for these people the essential Christian event. Their restoration, then, would be a restoration of the Pentecost phenomenon which began the Christian story.

Preoccupation with primitive Christianity, and especially with the day of Pentecost, abounds in the records of early Pentecostalism. The movement began at Charles Parham's Bethel College in Topeka, Kansas, where a student, Agnes Ozman, manifested the gift of tongues on New Year's Eve, 1900. Others in the Bethel group, meeting in an "upper room," soon began to speak in other languages as well. As Robert Mapes Anderson, one of Pentecostalism's leading historians, observes, this scenario was "almost exactly as pentecost is described in the second chapter of Acts."

The Pentecostals' self-conscious fascination with apostolic origins is illustrated by the titles of some of their periodicals: *The New Acts, Apostolic Messenger, Apostolic Evangel, The Pentecostal Record,* and *Pentecostal Wonders.* Indeed B. F. Lawrence, an elder in the Assemblies of God, contrasted Pentecostalism with the older denominations which had originated at particular points in Christian history.

> The Pentecostal Movement has no such history; it leaps the intervening years crying, *"Back to Pentecost."* In the minds of these honest-hearted, thinking men and women, this work of God is immediately connected with the work of God in New Testament days. Built by the same hand, upon the same foundation of apostles and prophets, after the same pattern, according to the same covenant, they too are a habitation of God through the Spirit. They do not recognize a doctrine or custom as authoritative unless it can be traced to that primal source of church instruction, the Lord and his apostles.

Perhaps in none of the Pentecostal sects was the restoration impulse more pronounced than in A. J. Tomlinson's Church of God based in Cleveland, Tennessee. Beginning as a Holiness community in a remote mountain region near the juncture of Tennessee, Georgia, and North Carolina, the Church of God embraced the doctrine of tongues in 1908. By 1910, Tomlinson was articulating the standard Pentecostal view of church history that the primitive church remained true to its original faith for a number of years but then "departed from the faith" and "was lost to view." Now in these latter days, however, the true church of God had been restored in the mountains of North Carolina and Tennessee.

Virtually all early Pentecostals spoke of restoration in the context of an imminent millennium. Recovery of pure beginnings, in fact, was inseparable from their awareness of living in the shadow of the end, an awareness that lent urgency to all their efforts to recover apostolic Christianity. In this, Pentecostals were reminiscent of both Alexander Campbell and Barton Stone, and even of Joseph Smith, the Mormon prophet.

Thus, A. J. Tomlinson taught that restoration of the primitive church in the mountains of North Carolina would eventually unify all Christians and hasten the millennial dawn. Likewise, B. F. Lawrence unflinchingly declared that "the last times are ushered in. The last days have come, in very truth. The harvest is at hand; nothing can stay the onward march of God and His glorious kingdom."

Their concern for first times (restoration) and last times (millennium) explains the Pentecostals' common "former rain"/ "latter rain" terminology (found originally in Deuteronomy 11:14, Joel 2:23, and James 5:7). The first Pentecost in Jerusalem was the "former rain" which launched the Christian age. Now, a second Pentecost—a "latter rain"—would conclude the Christian age just prior to the millennial era.

As the *Latter Rain Evangel* put it in 1909, "the first Pentecost *started* the church, . . . the second Pentecost *unites* and *perfects* the church unto the coming of the Lord." Sometimes the terminology was "morning light"/"evening light." Thus A. J. Tomlinson compared "the full blaze of light [which] beamed forth from the Pentecostal chamber" in the primitive church with his own age when "the evening light, the true light is now shining." But whatever the metaphor, the conviction remained constant that God was restoring the primitive church in these latter days and thereby hastening the millennial age.

Conclusion

Numerous denominations have grown from the Holiness/ Pentecostal revival. It should be said, first, that Holiness churches

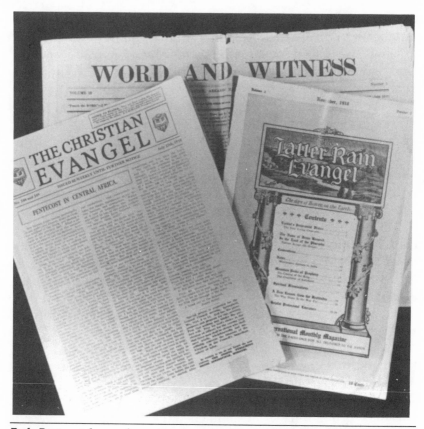

Early Pentecostal magazines: one announces a "Pentecost in Central Africa." (Assemblies of God Archives, Springfield, Missouri)

are not Pentecostal. Holiness denominations insist on sanctification as a second work of grace but do not believe in the Pentecostal experience of speaking in tongues. Major Holiness bodies today include the Church of the Nazarene and the Church of God (Anderson, Indiana).

On the other hand, Pentecostal churches embrace sanctification as a second work of grace and spiritual manifestations such as speaking in tongues as a third work of grace. Important Pentecostal denominations today include the Assemblies of God, the Church of God in Christ, and the Church of God (Cleveland, Tennessee).

Clearly, founders of both persuasions viewed primitive Christianity as providing the model for the church in their time.

Further, like Campbell and Stone, Holiness and Pentecostal teachers believed that restoration of primitive Christianity would prompt unity of all Christians and hasten the millennial age.

There, however, similarities break down. For while Alexander Campbell preached a rational restoration which would reproduce the forms and structures of the primitive church, the Holiness and Pentecostal advocates preached a restoration of openness to the Spirit of God. For them, holy living prompted by the Spirit's empowerment was seminal; forms, structures, and doctrinal intricacies were of less importance.

Questions

1. What was the central thrust of early Methodism as taught by John Wesley and as practiced by early Methodists on the American frontier?

2. How can one account for the increasing worldliness in America's Protestant churches in the years following the Civil War? Are there parallels between that period and our own age?

3. What prompted Holiness advocates in the late nineteenth century to leave the Methodist Church and organize separate "Holiness" denominations?

4. How did Holiness advocates define "the first work of grace"? "The second work of grace"?

5. What was the central focus of the restoration plea as it was stated by Holiness advocates? Was their emphasis in this regard biblical? What might Churches of Christ learn from the holiness understanding of restoration? What should Churches of Christ reject in the holiness understanding of restoration?

6. When Holiness advocates pointed to Holy Ghost baptism as the only basis for Christian union, what deeper conviction was implied regarding the relation between God and humankind?

7. Explain two reasons why Pentecostals were concerned to seek the gifts of the Spirit.

8. What was the central focus of the restoration plea as stated by Pentecostals? Was their emphasis in this regard biblical? What might Churches of Christ learn from the Pentecostals' understanding of restoration? What should Churches of Christ reject in the Pentecostals' understanding of restoration?

9. What was the meaning and significance of the "former rain"/ "latter rain" terminology among early Pentecostals?

For Further Study

Anderson, Robert Mapes. *Vision of the Disinherited: The Making of American Pentecostalism*. Oxford: Oxford University Press, 1979.

Dayton, Donald. *Theological Roots of Pentecostalism*. Grand Rapids: Zondervan, 1987.

Keefer, Luke L., Jr. "John Wesley: Disciple of Early Christianity." *Wesleyan Theological Journal* 19 (Spring 1984):23–35.

*Outler, Albert C. "'Biblical Primitivism' in Early American Methodism." In *The American Quest for the Primitive Church*. Edited by Richard T. Hughes. Urbana: University of Illinois Press, 1988.

Smith, Timothy L. *Called Unto Holiness: The Story of the Nazarenes*. Kansas City: Nazarene Publishing House, 1962.

Synan, Vinson. *The Holiness-Pentecostal Movement in the United States*. Grand Rapids: Eerdmans, 1971.

*Wacker, Grant. "Playing for Keeps: The Primitivist Impulse in Early Pentecostalism." In *The American Quest for the Primitive Church*.

13/Conclusion: What Can We Learn?

"Those who believe that they have no creed but the Bible will ... be victimized by the past. So too will those ... who believe that the history of the world begins with the birth of their own consciousness."

DAVID STEINMETZ (1976)

We began this book with the story of Jimmy, the fifty year old seaman suffering from a devastating loss of memory. His sad, almost unimaginable disorientation, we suggested, provides vivid testimony to the place memory occupies in a meaningful existence. Memory orients us within time, thereby providing identity and direction.

We believe the same holds true for the individual Christian and for the church as a whole. By "remembering" our spiritual ancestors and drawing them into our own circle of discourse, we gain rich and invigorating new perspectives on just who we are and where we need to go.

Now in this final chapter we reflect further on what we can learn from these mostly forgotten ancestors. We ask once more the questions with which we began: Why bother with tracing our "profane" or human roots? How do we come to terms with our tradition without simply denying that we have one? And how do we deal with the sense of finitude that a sympathetic reading of the past stirs within us?

Enlarging Our Circle of Discourse

One of the first and most basic things we can learn is simply the value of including the dead in our circle of discourse and thereby, as Jaroslav Pelikan noted, "enriching the quality of the conversation." The lesson is a hard one, however, especially for restorationists. For restorationism, as we have seen, often begets a sense of historylessness, an identification with the first century church so strong that the intervening history becomes irrelevant or even abhorent. History must be swept away, the polluted stream abandoned for the pure spring. Why listen, then, to those perceived as purveyors of confusion, apostates and blind guides, and voices of corruption? Why draw up chairs for them to join our enlightened conversation?

Such attitudes make it hard to listen openly and respectfully to voices from the past, even when those voices come from restorationists of a much earlier time who share our suspicion of the past. But as we do listen, such attitudes change. They change as we face Christians from the past and listen, however skeptically, to their ideas and share, however reluctantly, in their spiritual struggles.

We have sought in this book to foster such conversation by enlarging our circle of discourse. First and foremost, we have enlarged the circle to include spokespersons for the stream of restorationist thought that began in the Protestant Reformation. We have followed that stream through the Puritan movement, through the early Baptists in America, through the frenzy for pure beginnings in the early decades of American nationhood, down to the Stone-Campbell movement of the nineteenth century.

In the process we have conversed with enough people to surround a good-sized conference table: Erasmus of Rotterdam, Huldreich Zwingli, Heinrich Bullinger, Martin Bucer, John Calvin, William Tyndale, Thomas Cartwright, John Cotton, Roger Williams, Isaac Backus, Shubal Stearns, James Graves, Joseph Smith, Barton Stone, and Alexander Campbell. All of these leaders believed that time had seriously corrupted the Christian way and that a great restoration was imperative. Toward that end, most of them, in one way or another, focused their sights on restoring the forms and structures of the primitive church.

But if these men shared a core of common concerns, they differed sharply at many points. And those differences raise a number of difficult questions. Most obviously, why did they view the forms and structures of the primitive church in so many different ways? Why were some presbyterians and some congregationalists? Why did some look to certain Old Testament models and others only to New Testament ones? Why did some insist on infant baptism and others insist just as strongly on believer's baptism? Why did some practice laying on of hands and footwashing and others view those biblical practices as superfluous? Why did some banish musical instruments from worship and others see their use as a matter of small consequence?

Such obvious questions lead us to other less obvious ones. What forces were at work besides the professed passion for following the Bible? How did the personalities and intellects of the leaders themselves—the temper of mind, the ambitions, the conflicts, the bitter and triumphant experiences—shape their view of things? And what was the impact of tradition and culture? Could they have risen entirely above such "profane" influences? Can we?

In addition to conversations with these men, we have engaged others who stood outside this stream of thought: Luther with his strong reservations about restoration of biblical forms and structures, Menno Simons and the early Anabaptists with their focus on separation of the church from the world, and Holiness/Pentecostal advocates who sought restoration of the Spirit's power.

The questions these believers raise within our circle of discourse may be harder to hear than the others. Their questions, in fact, may sound strange or even threatening.

Luther asks: How, with your sights fixed on biblical forms, structures, and patterns, can you keep from overshadowing the gospel of grace which alone gives life? Do you think the church on earth must be perfect, and that you must be the ones to make it so? Do external marks alone constitute the church? Or does the church not exist wherever people hear Christ preached and respond with faith?

The Anabaptists ask: Why, with all your apostolic forms and practices, do you live so comfortably at home in a corrupt and transient world? Are not moral purity and brotherly love truer marks of a Christian community than saying the right words and going through the proper motions?

And the Holiness/Pentecostal advocates ask: How can one talk about biblical Christianity at all while neglecting the very power of godliness—the Spirit's work? Does salvation and the life of holiness depend upon human intellect and will power or upon a Power from beyond ourselves renewing our minds and invigorating our wills?

With such questions the circle of discourse, we realize, may become a circle of discord. But still we must listen. As Karl Barth put it, Christians

> must be strong enough and free enough to listen quietly, attentively, and openly to the voices not merely of the classical past but of all the past .... We cannot anticipate which co-workers of the past will be welcome in our own work, and which not. It may always be that those unexpected and even unwelcome voices will be the ones we particularly need.

Coming to Terms with Tradition

By enlarging our circle of discourse we can better address the inescapable problem of tradition. As we saw in the first chapter, we cannot escape tradition no matter how hard we might try; rather, we face the choice of being "unconscious victims or conscious participants."

Restorationists most often fail to appreciate this fact, however. And understandably so. For they see little but the treachery of tradition. They see how quickly tradition grows moribund, stifling living faith, fostering schism, and compromising with the world. So they want nothing to do with it. They want only the truth—fresh, timeless, and culture-free.

The sweeping rejection of tradition, however, results not in a traditionless and culture-free faith but in a faith even more vulnerable to blind traditionalism. It results, as we have seen repeatedly throughout this book, in powerful traditions propelled by the illusion of existing without tradition. It results in the easy assumption that one's roots are simply sacred and biblical, not in any way "profane" and cultural. With such an assumption a restoration movement easily accumulates an array of full-blown traditions, most of which remain invisible under the traditional rhetoric of scorning tradition.

We repeat: human traditions are simply inevitable, even among those—or perhaps *especially* among those—who reject them. We would do well, therefore, to admit it, for only then can we begin the self-conscious engagement with tradition so vital to a healthy church. Tradition, we must recognize, is always a mixed blessing: it easily domesticates and distorts the Christian way, to be sure, but it also conserves and sustains it.

What are some of our traditions? An important one, clearly, is the way we conceive the task of restoration itself. As we have seen, Churches of Christ stand in a stream of thought—a tradition—focusing on the restoration of churchly forms and structures. To put it more strongly, we have often proceeded on the assumption that if one did not focus attention on biblical form and structure then one was actually neither a restorationist nor biblical at all, and perhaps not even Christian.

Another tradition, undergirding the first, is a particular way of interpreting the Bible. Central to this interpretive method has been the insistence that the Bible needs little if any interpretation. Tolbert Fanning, founding editor of the *Gospel Advocate*, put it starkly when he claimed that the Scriptures are "but a transcript of the mind of our Heavenly Father" and, when fairly translated, "need no explanation." The implications were clear: whereas humanly devised denominations impose their interpretation upon the Bible and distort it, we among Churches of Christ do not interpret the Bible at all—we simply read it the way God wrote it. Such a view, ironically, allows traditional and cultural assumptions about Scripture to operate behind the scenes, shaping our interpretation unconsciously.

Many other traditions, varying from place to place and time to time, cluster around these two basic ones. A typical list from a few years back might include a "Word only" view of the Spirit, the five steps of salvation, use of invitation hymns, a "low church" worship style, exclusive use of one particular version or translation, a disproportionate focus on Acts of the Apostles and certain Pauline epistles, and opposition to (take your pick) racial integration, racial segregation, church cooperation, church non-cooperation, long hair on men, short hair on women, etc.

We are not suggesting a rejection of all our traditions. That would be disorienting and difficult. And of course we are not suggesting a bland acquiescence to them. That would be disastrous. We are suggesting simply that we recognize the inevitable fact of tradition so that, with clearer vision, we can examine our lives and our congregations in the clear and constant light of God's Word.

Facing Our Finitude

Coming to terms with tradition inevitably forces us to face our finitude, our status as time-bound, culture-bound, sinful members of the human race. We face our finitude at two levels: singly, as individuals, and together, as a people who call themselves the church.

As individuals, a sympathetic listening to voices from the past should elicit a basic confession: that we are beset by blindnesses and weaknesses fully as acute as those which afflicted past believers whose errors we think we see so clearly and whom we judge so easily. By thinking otherwise we succumb to what C. S. Lewis called "chronological snobbery"—the conceit that we somehow are wiser, more heroic, more clear-headed, or more reasonable than our spiritual forebearers.

Of course, we seek to learn from our ancestors' blindnesses and struggles on behalf of the faith—they would want us to—but in many ways we seldom if ever surpass them. In combining scholarship with devotion, for example, we are hard-pressed to equal Erasmus. In proclaiming the glories of God's grace, we could hardly surpass Luther. In courage, most of us pale beside William Tyndale and Menno Simons. In joining conviction with tolerance, we have many lessons to learn from Roger Williams. And in the passion for a pure church, not many of us match John Cotton and the Puritans.

With all of them, however, we share equally in a common humanity. As that common humanity dawns upon us from time to time, most often something else happens: a deeper sense of God's grace—the expanse and wonder of it—dawns upon us as well.

Besides confronting us with our humanness as individuals, our glimpse into the past also confronts us with the human shape of the church. It forces us to recognize the great disparity between the ideal and the actual, between the church as a theological doctrine and as a social reality, a divine institution and a human one.

Among Churches of Christ, we have had difficulty making such distinctions. Though holding a high vision of a glorious and divinely perfect church, we have not faced up well to a human and painfully imperfect church—the one we meet with on Sundays and spend our lives struggling with and loving. Those of us in

Churches of Christ often have lived in a historical vacuum where, exempt from the tides of time that ebb and flow against all earthly institutions, we easily assume that the church is not human at all but only divine. From such an assumption it is only a small step to a smug and self-righteous perfectionism. There follows close behind an insidious blindness permitting the ever-present forces of tradition and culture to do their work undetected and thus uncontrolled.

The tension between the church as human and divine and between present hope and future fulfillment appears clearly in the biblical imagery of the church as Christ's body (Eph. 1:22–23; Col. 1:18, 2:19) and Christ's bride (Eph. 5:25–27; Col. 1:22, 28; 2 Cor. 11:2). As Eric Jay comments:

> Body and head are not identical; the bride is not the bridegroom; the Church is not the Christ. There is a tension of thought here: integrated unity, yet not identity. In its unity with Christ the Church shares in his glory and perfection . . . but it is far from glory and perfection . . . . The Church is holy; the church is to become holy.

We need to reclaim this tension. We have often proclaimed "The Glorious Church" while forgetting that, though it partakes of Christ's glory and fullness, it will be wholly glorious, wholly "without spot and wrinkle," only when Christ returns to wash it clean and "present the church to himself" (Eph. 5:26–27). Meanwhile we struggle toward and live in hope of that perfection. We must see the glory, to be sure. But we must see with equal clarity its absence so that we can ever strive toward it.

Augustine of Hippo, the great Christian theologian of the fifth century, often described the church as without spot and wrinkle. But he realized toward the end of his life that the description was inadequate and that he could only pray, "Forgive us our sins."

What can we learn from tracing our spiritual roots? Among many things, especially this: that God sustains the church by grace just as God saves sinners by grace. Remembering that, we will remember who we are, whose we are, and where our hope lies.

Questions

1. Which person or movement treated in this book has proved most meaningful in your own "circle of discourse"? Why?

2. How would you explain the many differences among those who sought restoration of the forms and structures of the primitive church? What does your explanation suggest for Churches of Christ today?

3. How do you respond to Luther's questions? To those of the Anabaptists? To those of Holiness/Pentecostal advocates?

4. Can restorationists come to terms with tradition without ceasing to be restorationists? Why or why not?

5. Make your own list of traditions important to Churches of Christ. Where did they come from and what should we do with them?

6. What are some of the ways this tracing of our roots has affected your thinking?

Index of Names

Age of Reason, 75-86, 138
Amish, 134
Ammann, Jakob, 134
Anabaptists, 7, 28, 29, 76, 110, 125-35, 137, 153
Anglican Church, 43-46, 50, 76, 138
Aquinas, Thomas, 12
Asbury, Francis, 102
Assemblies of God, 148
Augustine of Hippo, 157

Backus, Isaac, 66, 67, 152
Bacon, Francis, 84
Baconianism, 84
Baptists, 3, 7, 56, 57, 63-72, 89, 93, 104, 110, 139
  General, 63
  Landmark, 69-72
  Particular, 63, 64
  Separate, 60, 65-68, 102-103
Barnes, Robert, 36
Barrow, Henry, 46
Barth, Karl, 154
Bay Psalm Book, 53-54
Brooks, John P., 141
Browne, Robert, 46
Bucer, Martin, 29, 30, 31, 39, 152
Bullinger, Heinrich, 29, 30, 39, 152

Calvin, John, 6, 30, 31-32, 33, 59, 127, 152
Campbell, Alexander, 3, 7, 33, 47, 60, 68, 69, 84, 85, 95-96, 106-109, 133, 134, 143, 147, 152
Campbell, Thomas, 33, 60, 80-82
Cane Ridge Revival, 102
Cartwright, Thomas, 43-45, 46, 152
Christian Association of Washington, 80, 106
Churches of Christ, 2, 6, 7, 11, 13, 21, 47, 71, 75, 78, 89-90, 94-95, 98, 101-10, 113, 133-34, 155-57
Church of God (Anderson, Indiana), 143, 148
Church of God (Cleveland, TN), 146, 148
Church of God in Christ, 148
Church of the Nazarene, 142, 143, 148
Coke, Thomas, 139
Colet, John, 36_

Common Sense Realism, 84, 106
Congregationalist Church, 93
Constantine, 29, 57, 76, 125-26
Cotton, John, 7, 51-57, 59, 152, 156
Cox, Richard, 32
Cranmer, Thomas, 39

Dayton, Amos, 70, 71
Deism, 77, 78
Dering, Edward, 45
Descartes, Rene, 83
Disciples of Christ, 109

Edward VI, 30, 38, 40
Edwards, Jonathan, 65
Edwards, Morgan, 64-65, 67
Elizabeth I, 41, 45
Elizabethan Settlement, 41
Enlightenment, 75-86, 106, 109, 133
Erasmus of Rotterdam, 11, 15, 17, 18, 19, 25, 26, 36, 38, 152, 156

Frith, John, 36

Glas, John, 47
Gordon, A. J., 140
Graves, James R., 63, 69-70, 105, 152
Great Awakening, 65
Grebel, Conrad, 27-29, 125, 128
Greenwood, John, 46
Grindal, Edmond, 45
Gutenberg Bible, 14

Haggard, Rice, 103
Haldane, James, 47
Hall, B. F., 85, 108
Harris, Robert Lee, 142, 143
Helwys, Thomas, 63
Henry VIII, 38
Herbert of Cherbury, Lord, 77-80, 82
Holiness movement, 110, 140-144, 154
Hooker, Richard, 43-45
Hooper, John, 39
Hubmaier, Balthasar, 131
Hus, John, 13, 59
Hutter, Jakob, 134

Jefferson, Thomas, 89, 90
Jewel, John, 41
Jones, Abner, 102

Karlstadt, Andreas Bodenstein von, 120

Knox, John, 32

Latimer, Hugh, 39
Laud, William, 49
Lawrence, B. F., 137, 146-47
Leland, John, 66
Levy, Edgar M., 143-44
Lewis, C. S., 1, 156
Lipscomb, David, 3
Locke, John, 7, 75, 78-80, 82, 106
Lollards, 13
Luther, Martin, 7, 23, 26, 28, 30, 36, 38, 59, 76, 110, 113-22, 127, 130, 153, 156
Lutheran tradition, 23, 76, 93

McCalla, W. L., 107
McNemar, Richard, 104

Marshal, Daniel, 67
Mary Tudor, 39, 40
Massachusetts Bay Colony, 50, 55, 57, 64
Methodist Church, 70, 71, 93, 102, 104, 138-40
More, Thomas, 15-16
Mormon, 89-90, 94-98, 105, 137, 143
Müntzer, Thomas, 27

New Testament Church of Christ, 142-43
Newton, Isaac, Sir, 83

O'Kelly, James, 101

Paine, Thomas, 90, 91
Parham, Charles, 145-46
Pelikan, Jaroslav, 4, 5
Penry, John, 46
Pentecostal movement, 110, 144-48, 154
Philadelphia Baptist Association, 64
Philips, Dietrich, 132
Pilgrims, 46
Pope, Alexander, 83
Presbyterian, 80, 93, 104, 106, 139
Puritans, 3, 7, 65, 66, 67, 79, 82, 106, 109, 110, 113
    English, 35-47, 49, 50, 63
    New England, 49-60

Quakers, 56, 93

Reformed tradition, 23, 24, 30, 31, 33, 35, 75, 93, 110, 113
Reid, Thomas, 84
Ridley, Nicholas, 39
Rigdon, Sidney, 95
Robinson, John, 35, 46
Rogers, John, 108
Roman Catholic Church, 12, 18, 23, 25, 27, 28, 35, 36, 42, 75, 76, 93, 117, 118, 134

Sacks, Oliver, 1
Sandeman, Robert, 47
Scott, Walter, 6, 7, 33
Shakers, 89
Shepard, Thomas, 55
Simons, Menno, 125, 130-32, 134, 153, 156
Smith, Elias, 101
Smith, Hannah Whitall, 144
Smith, Joseph, 94-96, 105, 147, 152
Smyth, John, 63
Springfield Presbytery, 102
Srygley, Fletcher, 140
Stearnes, Shubal, 67, 152
Stewart, Dugald, 84
Stone, Barton, 3, 6, 7, 33, 68, 96, 101-105, 107-108, 147, 152
Stone-Campbell Movement, 7, 11, 68, 96-97, 143

Theodosius, 76, 126
Tindal, Mathew, 83
Toland, John, 83
Tomlinson, A. J., 146-47
Tyndale, William, 35-38, 40, 46, 76, 152, 156

United Church of Christ, 102

Warner, Daniel S., 143, 144
Wesley, John, 138-39, 141
Whitefield, George, 65
Whitgift, John, 45
Williams, Roger, 7, 56-60, 64, 95, 156
Winthrop, John, 50, 59
Wittenberg movement, 119-20
Wyclif, John, 13, 59

Zwingli, Huldreich, 6, 21, 24-29, 33, 41, 44, 127-28, 152
Zwinglians, 3, 76